from HAVANA to DC:
The Rise of Cuban Americans in Florida Politics

CARLOS F. ORTA

For More Information:

Carlos F. Orta | www.havanatodc.com
Fig Factor Media | www.figfactormedia.com
Cover Design and Layout by LDG Juan Manuel Serna Rosales

Printed in the United States of America

ISBN: 978-1-959989-74-5
Library of Congress Control Number: 2024906523

Dedication

From Havana to DC: The Rise of Cuban Americans in Florida Politics came from conversations I had with my wife, Mary Ann, over many dinners. Most of these conversations happened when we were quarantined because of Covid-19 in Chevy Chase, MD in 2020 and 2021.

As I shared these stories with her over many dinners, she kept telling me, "You were part of that history, those historic moments. You need to write about that."

I never thought of it in that way, that I was part of history. I guess when you're in the middle of it, you don't think about it that way. Not only was I a witness to this history, but I had a front row seat, and along with a lot of friends, I was part of the history. I was there, working with the history makers themselves.

Mary Ann made me look at my time and participation, and that of the others, in a historical way. She really inspired me to write this book, and so I dedicate it to her.

I also dedicate the book to my parents, Carlos and Maria Luisa Orta. Because of them, I have had a most wonderful life that would never have been possible in a Communist Cuba.

The next dedication extends to the many friends who were part of my growing up in Florida politics and sharing those experiences with them.

Friends like Rocky Egusquiza, Alex Fernandez, Ana Carbonell, Carlos Cruz, Ana Carbonell, Annette Molina, Isabel Cosio, Richard Candia, David R. Custin, Edgar Fernandez, Joe Fraga, Virginia Sanchez, Miguel Otero, Jose K. Fuentes, Gloria Oliveros, Millie Ruiz, Rick Rodriguez Piña, Lenys Klumpp, Ralph O. Rodriguez, Maria Ines Castro, Marisel Manteiga, Joyce Postell, Maribel Balbin, Carlos Manriquez, Jorge Luis Lopez, Marisol Rodriguez, Sergio Abreu, Gene Wilk, Rana Brown, Kendrick Meek, Marilu Escobar, Omar Franco, Kathleen Sullivan, Edgar Duarte, Bonnie Michaels, Marian P. Johnson and so many others who are mentioned or included in the book.

Apologies to those that my memory failed to capture.

Special shout out to Maytee Sanz, whose offer of a summer internship during a challenging, rough spot in my life, completely changed the trajectory of my career and life, and for the best!

To Miguel de Grandy for believing in me, when I did not, and being there for me when I needed that extra push. To Nilo Juri for taking a big chance when hiring me.

The last dedication goes to the new generation of young, bright political professionals, legislative aides, and operatives who are starting out and wondering about their future. Those that are making, and at the same time, being part of today's history. Rest assured that if you have a strong moral compass, you will be more successful than you can imagine in the "business of politics."

Table of Contents

Acknowledgments

Putting yourself out there by writing a book such as this can be intimidating, especially for an introvert like me. Once the manuscript was 80/90 percent completed, I needed to share it with individuals whose opinions I valued, Cuban American and non-Cubans.

A little more than half a dozen individuals read the manuscript, and all provided great advice, suggestions, and counsel. Changes were made, paragraphs taken out, and new ones written. Gracias go out to:

- Guarione Diaz, former CEO, Cuban American National Council (CNC)
- Alfredo Estrada, Editor and Publisher, *LATINO* Magazine
- Rocky Egusquiza, Executive Director, Latin GRAMMY Cultural Foundation
- Frank Gómez, Partner, Latin Insights
- David Lawrence, Jr., former Editor and Publisher, *The Miami Herald*
- Daniel Neep, Professor, Georgetown University
- Raúl R. Tapia, Washington, D.C., Attorney, Businessman and Lobbyist

Advice and Counsel:
- Dr. Juana Bordas, Mestiza Leadership International
- Humberto Cortina, Former State Representative
- Monica Diaz, Author, *From Intent to Impact: The 5 Dualities of Diversity and Inclusion*
- Jose K. Fuentes from Becker, who connected me with everyone I asked of him. It was a lot!
- Raul Martinez, Jr. and David Damron from Congresswoman Debbie Wasserman Schultz's office
- Leslie Sanchez, CBS News Political Commentator & Executive Producer, *Insider Game* Documentary series
- Adis Villa, Friend, lifelong mentor & Board Member, Latino Corporate Directors Association

To my publisher, Jacqueline "Jackie" Ruiz, CEO, JJR Marketing, so proud to have worked with such a pro and a fierce Latina!

Foreword
From Havana to DC: A Legacy of Freedom

In the heart of Florida, a political saga unfolds, one forged in the crucible of exile and fueled by an unyielding desire for freedom. This is the story of Cuban Americans, a community whose rise to power has reshaped the Sunshine State and sent shockwaves across the nation's political landscape.

Beyond the sun-drenched beaches and vibrant salsa beats lies a story of unwavering determination. It's a tale whispered in hushed tones, etched in the hearts of those who fled the iron grip of Castro's Cuba. From whispers of Bill Clinton blaming Cubans for his electoral loss to the chilling "treacherous individual" haunting Al Gore's campaign trail, this book delves into the shadows and secrets that have propelled Cuban Americans to the forefront of American politics.

Yet, this is not merely a chronicle of political intrigue. Carlos Orta masterfully explores the soul of a community bound by shared history and a singular dream: a free Cuba. From the Bay of Pigs to the Mariel Boatlift, Orta traces the threads that bind them, understanding how each exile, each sacrifice, has woven itself into the fabric of their political identity.

Miami, once a sleepy coastal town, has become a potent symbol of their ascendance. We witness its transformation, fueled by demographic shifts and the relentless ambition of a community that has carved its own destiny. Carlos introduces us to the pioneers, the first Cuban Americans to break down barriers, their stories told through the eyes of someone who walked beside them, a legislative aide who witnessed history unfold in the corridors of power.

But the story doesn't end there. Orta interviews Democrats and Republicans, veterans and newcomers, all bound by the shared legacy of exile. We hear their voices, their hopes, and their fears in candid interviews, understanding the complexities that define their geopolitical influence.

Orta's book is not just about politics; it's about the human spirit. It's about the power of resilience, the unwavering belief in a dream that transcends borders and generations. This is the story of Cuban Americans, a story etched in search of freedom, whispered in dreams, and forever shaping an ever-changing America.

Leslie Sanchez *is a media entrepreneur, respected author, and award-winning CBS News political analyst. Previously she served as the Executive Director of the White House Initiative on Hispanic Education under the George W. Bush Administration.*

Introduction

For a while now, I have wanted to write a book about my life and adventures, a semi-autobiographical type of book. In the summer of 2020, a few months into the Covid-19 pandemic, I began to write that book. It was then that I realized that I could write another book about "growing up" in Florida politics as it coincided with the rise of Cuban Americans in Florida politics.

With the exception of a few years, as I was working in Florida politics, Cuban Americans were making history, going from zero elected Cuban Americans in the Florida Legislature in 1980, to the election of almost two dozen by the year 2000.

WHY THIS BOOK?

This is my "love letter" to the first group of Cuban Americans who were appointed or elected to political and public office and who I was fortunate enough to know or work with.

For my friends, my family, my community, and for this and the next generations to come of young political operatives and legislative aides. For the political junkies, and all those that love the sport of politics. For the love of bipartisanship.

WHY NOW?

Because it is a story that has not been told, and it needs to, I feel. The story now spans more than 60 years, two generations since Fidel Castro's takeover of Cuba on January 1, 1959.

It is a small number of Cuban Americans, the first elected to local, state, and federal office, who are responsible for the dozens that have followed in their footsteps. Most of the individuals included in the book are still alive, living their best lives after making history and setting the standard for public service.

LOOKING FORWARD

Lastly, it is important to remind the readers, including the new generation of Cuban America elected and appointed officials, of the history and what has transpired, and how far we've come and how much further we can go!

For me personally, I've been greatly impacted, personally and professionally, in a most awesome way, by public service and politics. I had no idea that a single political internship in the summer of 1988 would completely change my trajectory.

It would change what I had envisioned being since I was 8 years old, an architect who wanted to build beach houses. And, regardless of where I've lived, being "Cuban" has always peaked people's interest and defined me.

To the Reader,

I hope you enjoy this book. As you do, keep in mind this is a semi-autobiographical work. In addition to relying on my own recollections, I did extensive research and spoke to many of the people featured in the book to ensure I recalled memories and incidents correctly, and ensured I did not miss anything, which I am sure I did. It was wonderful re-connecting with all of them. Being Cuban, there could be some exaggerations and recollections that are not 100% spot on.

With much love & respect,

Carlos

Me, at the age of five, celebrating my birthday in Madrid, Spain.
To this day, I still enjoy a nice, cold glass of Coke!

L-R: Barry Coughlin (Ford), me with then Miami-Dade County Mayor Alex Penelas and State Senator Mario Díaz-Balart, circa 1998 or 1999.

Me, my mom and her sisters/my aunts at my graduation party from Barry University, 1995.

About the Author

I was born in Havana, Cuba, on Friday, June 3, 1966. The only child of Carlos and Maria Luisa Orta. In Cuba, Mom was a schoolteacher and Dad was a Certified Public Accountant. I grew up in the most western part of Cuba, a town called Pinar del Rio, whose claim to fame is the production of the all-revered, all-mighty Cuban cigar.

In 1969, we left Cuba on "vacation" and ended up in Madrid, Spain, where we sought political asylum. We lived in Madrid for a couple of years until we had the resources to come to the United States.

In August of 1971, we landed at JFK International Airport and began to make our way to Miami, Florida, where I could meet my family (mom's and dad's) for the first time. It was also the first time that I realized that I was different from all my cousins because I only spoke Spanish, and Castilian Spanish at that. I also realized that while I could see some of my favorite TV shows I'd watched in Madrid, I could not understand them because they were in English. This was very traumatic for me, and it has always stayed with me, yet I don't know why.

*Me and my favorite cousin shortly after arriving
in Miami in the summer of 1971.*

We first lived in Little Havana (corner of 6th Street and 12th Avenue) in a roach-infested rented apartment. I would say that I had what most would classify as a typical "Cuban American middle class" upbringing. Both of my parents worked a lot, so I spent a lot of time with my mother's mom. She often lived with us, or I spent a lot of time at her apartment. She is really the one who raised me during the early years.

Dad, Mom, Me, girl cousins, family friend, Grandmother and little cousin, circa 1972.

In 1973, my parents bought their first and only home in what today is known as West Miami. My mom still lives in the house. The American Dream was achieved!

For the first few years after my parents bought the house until I was in 7th or 8th grade, our family was the only Cubans on our block. Our neighbors and, by default, neighborhood friends – Troy, Sheri, Jude, and Jaime – were "Gringos or Americanos." It is from them that my love of rock & roll music, really, all things "American" come from.

At school, it was a different story. There, the majority of my school chums were Cuban Americans. It was interesting being able to go back and forth between the two cultures. And as a result, I understood the importance of being able to "walk" in both worlds and be seen as legitimate. Some of my friends were not able to do that. I was definitely Cuban; I was definitely American—and uniquely Cuban-American.

Until 6th grade, I attended public schools. From 7th through 12th grade, I attended Miami Private School, a small, private school run by a former Cuban political prisoner who did not hesitate to use a paddle to get us to a remorseful state, rather quickly, when we misbehaved.

I enjoyed my high school years. Going to a small private school—our graduating class was 35, the largest in the school's history—allowed you to make some really great friendships as most of the 7th graders I started with, I graduated with.

BURSTING THE BUBBLE

Since the time I was around 8-9 years old, I had always wanted to be an architect. It would have been nice if someone had burst my bubble by explaining to me that you needed to be pretty good in math. I have sucked at math since 2th grade.

After graduating high school in 1984, I immediately enrolled at Miami-Dade Community College (MDCC), now called Miami-Dade College (MDC), a two-year educational institution. Sort of a transition spot between high school and going to the university for kids who either didn't have their act together or couldn't get into a university right after high school. That would be me! As I think about it, I never had a discussion with my parents about applying for universities outside of Miami. It was neither an option nor up for discussion.

Four years after graduating high school, I was still at MDCC. I was not a good student. My MDCC transcripts backs this up. Eventually, I did complete my 60 credits at MDCC and transferred to Barry University, where I earned a Bachelor of Liberal Arts. I graduated in the summer of 1995, 11 years after graduating high school. During those 11 years, I worked in politics, both as an operative and a legislative aide.

MY JOURNEY INTO POLITICS AND PUBLIC SERVICE

In the summer of 1988, I received a phone call that would completely change the trajectory of what I had envisioned as a career. A high school friend of mine, Maytee Sanz, was working as a legislative aide for a very popular and influential Florida State Senator named Ileana Ros-Lehtinen. I don't recall exactly how we connected, but when we did, she offered me a summer internship, which I accepted and, as they say, the rest is history.

From 1988 until the summer of 2004, I excelled at political campaigns, working for elected and appointed officials, and eventually becoming a lobbyist at two Fortune 500 companies: Waste Management, Inc and Ford Motor Company. I traveled extensively through Florida and then throughout the U.S. with Ford, ending up as a Regional Manager responsible for an 11-state region, based in Kansas City, MO.

In the fall of 2004, Anheuser-Busch recruited me to manage their community relations and philanthropic giving in Arizona, Nevada, and California. I relocated from the Midwest to Los Angeles, CA—one of two cities I had always wanted to live in. Washington, D.C., being the other.

In 2006, I moved to Washington, D.C., to run the Hispanic Association on Corporate Responsibility (HACR). I led HACR until February 2014, when I accepted a job with Carnival Corporation as Vice President of Corporate Affairs. While in D.C., I met Mary Ann Gomez who, at the time, was the Executive Director at the National Association of Hispanic Publications, a national Hispanic nonprofit.

While CEO of HACR, attending a meeting with NBC News executives Natalie Morales, Steve Capus, Brian Williams and Ann Curry, in NYC. Also pictured are Janet Murguia, me and two Chicago area Latino leaders.

Mary Ann and I were married on September 4, 2016, in Palm Beach, Florida in front of a small group of friends and family, on the beach. After Carnival, she and I relocated back to Washington, D.C., where I had accepted a job with a Latino nonprofit. Little did we know it was just in time for Covid-19, and that's when I began work on this book.

November 7, 2015. Proposal Day. New York City's Centra Park, The Great Lawn.

It's been a wonderful experience. Nothing like I've ever experienced before. It has been wonderful to reconnect with longtime friends, acquaintances and meet new folks. I have enjoyed doing a lot of research, which would often bring back memories I had forgotten about. Same for the many folks that I have written about, who I connected with as I was writing the book.

I am not sure where life takes me after the publication of the book, but I have no doubt it will be fun and exciting. And I am really excited to meet many of you at book signings, book fairs, and local bookstores.

Chapter 1
CUBA AND CUBANS: A PRIMER

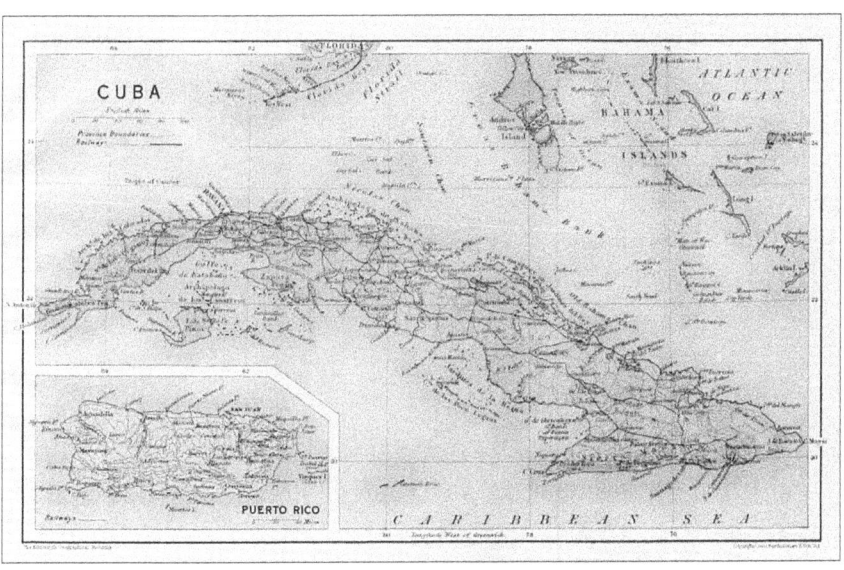

I feel so fortunate to have been born in Havana, Cuba, the largest and certainly one of the most beautiful islands in the Caribbean, or the world for that matter. It is a place of rich history, traditions and wonderful people. I also feel equally fortunate and very privileged to have had been raised in the United States, and in particular, Miami, Florida.

I am a proud product of both, and both have defined who I am. We, Cuban Americans love our freedom, and we have paid a high price for it. We love America—land of the free, home of the brave, and at the same time, we love our country of origin just as much, if not more.

Cubans can be a complicated group to know or understand, and Cuba's proximity to the U.S. often adds to that complexity. As such, I felt it was important to start my book with what I call a "primer" on Cuba and Cubans.

As Cuban exiles, we have faced much adversity in our fight for a free Cuba: the embargo, the Bay of Pigs invasion, Pedro Pan Freedom Flights, and the 1980 Mariel Boatlift, among others. I'll briefly shed some light on these traumatic situations in hopes they serve as insights into who Cubans are and how these events have affected our views and our politics. These situations have allowed us to transform a once, sleepy, non-diverse tourist town into a global powerhouse, the gateway to Latin American and the Caribbean, and one of the sexiest cities in the world.

I've also asked some special contributors to chime in on their thoughts, so you can read other perspectives. While Cuban Americans are found all over the U.S., my focus for this book are those based in South Florida, i.e., Miami-Dade County. The ones I grew up with, politically speaking. The ones who made Cuban and American history by becoming the first elected and appointed to government and political offices.

I do briefly mention Cubans outside of Miami, because they, too, were the "firsts" in their respective locations; but the real focus is Miami, Florida. No offense is meant to other "Cuban" cities or individuals.

Lastly, several books delve much deeper into what I have written about in the first few chapters. I encourage you to do deeper dives on what most interests you. If you still yearn to learn more, please visit go to the Pew Research Center where you will find abundant information on my people. So does FIU CasaCuba, The Cuban Heritage Collection at the University of Miami, Barry University (on Operation Peter Pan), Miami Dade College, and Facts About Cuban Exiles (www.facecuba.org), just to name a few.

Bottom line: This book—and the first few chapters—should help you understand the complexity of the Cuban American community, and its simplicity as well. For it is both complex and simple, and you will come to appreciate why attaining political power was crucial to the Cuban community in our collective fight for a "Free Cuba."

CUBA'S ORIGINS

On October 27, 1492, Christopher Columbus landed on the north coast of Cuba and immediately took possession of it on behalf of the Spanish monarchs, naming it Juana in honor of the Spanish princess. According to his diary, Columbus declared Cuba "the most beautiful land that human eyes have ever seen" and called its inhabitants "Indians," thinking he had arrived in India. For 300 years under Spanish rule, Cuba remained a less important part of the Spanish empire and was used primarily as a naval supply base for Spanish fleets, transporting gold and silver from Mexico and Perú.

In 1762-63, the British occupied Cuba. According to Cubahistory. com, "Two days after the declaration of war with Spain, on the advice of Lord Anson, the British cabinet chose Havana as a major objective in its attack on Spain because of its strategic importance, believing that its permanent loss would weaken Spanish influence in the Caribbean." Oppressive Spanish trade restrictions were lifted, and Cuba was thrown open to trade with England and its North American colonies. Following the British occupation, Spain relaxed its restrictive trade policies and allowed Cubans to trade with its neighbors to the north, giving Cuba an initial economic impulse.

With the slave uprising and the destruction of the sugar plantations in neighboring Haiti in the 1790s, Cuba was ready to become the sugar bowl of the Caribbean and replace Haiti as the supplier of sugar to Europe. Thousands of slaves were imported to work the sugar plantations. Throughout the 19th century, sugar, coffee, and tobacco became increasingly important. Large cattle estates were subdivided, and the Spanish government aided the development of sugar. In 1795, Cuba had 478 sugar mills. By 1860, it is estimated that over 900 steam sugar mills were together producing over 500,000 tons of sugar.

FREEDOM FROM SPANISH RULE

The sugar mills enabled the growth of a prosperous and influential class of rural proprietors had emerged. This new wealthy aristocracy feared a repetition in Cuba of the events in Haiti; they supported the Spanish monarchy and sought the army's protection.

One of the warriors who most valiantly fought for Cuba's freedom and shared the ideals of independence was Lt. General Antonio Maceo, a mulato born in Santiago de Cuba in 1845. He and Máximo Gómez, a general of the Cuban Army of Dominican origin, led the Cubans in the famous machete charges that helped undermine Spanish power.

Yet, the most important leader of Cuba's independence struggle was José Martí, a poet, philosopher, essayist, journalist, translator, professor, publisher, and so much more. Through his writings and political activism, Martí became a symbol of Cuba's bid for independence from Spain in the 19th century and is often referred to as the "Apostle of Cuban Independence."

Martí traveled extensively in Spain, Latin America, and the United States, raising awareness of and support for the cause of Cuban independence. His unification of the Cubans in Florida and in New York City, where an equestrian statue of him graces the entrance to Central Park on West 59th Street, was crucial to the success of the Cuban War of Independence against Spain. He was a key civilian figure, politically and financially, in the planning and execution of this war, as well as the designer of the Cuban Revolutionary Party and its ideology. He died in battle during the Battle of Dos Ríos on May 19, 1895.

THE TREATY OF PARIS OF 1898

On December 10, 1898, the United States and Spain signed the Treaty of Paris which, in effect, ended the Spanish-American War. The treaty required Spain to relinquish "all claim of sovereignty over and title to Cuba, Puerto Rico, Guam, and the Philippines to the U.S." The cession of the Philippines involved a compensation of $20M from the U.S. to Spain. It has been said that the Treaty of Paris marked the end of the Spanish Empire and the beginning of the United States as a world power.

THE U.S. AND CUBA

The three-year U.S. occupation of Cuba produced numerous changes. It revived the economy, created a system of rural guards, and a new Cuban army. Health and education received much attention. Yellow fever was eradicated primarily through the work of Cuban scientist Carlos J. Finlay who discovered that mosquitoes transmitted the disease. The Americans established a sanitation system, a public school system, reorganized the judicial system, and helped draft the 1901 Cuban Constitution. The U.S. included in the Constitution the Platt Amendment giving the U.S. the right to intervene in Cuba. A serious setback to Cuba's nationalistic ideals.

According to a *Cubans in America* article:

> In 1902, the U.S. ended its occupation, and Cuba launched into nationhood with fewer problems than most Latin American nations. Prosperity increased during the early years, militarism seemed curtailed, and social tensions were not profound. However, corruption, violence, and political irresponsibility grew. A second United States intervention and economic involvement weakened the growth of Cuban nationality and made Cuba more dependent on its northern neighbor.
>
> The 1930s saw a major attempt at revolution, prompted by Gerardo Machado's cruel dictatorship, the economic hardships of the world depression, the growing control of the economy by Spaniards and North Americans, and a series of international events that included the Soviet and Mexican revolutions and student revolts in Latin America.

Chapter 2
MODERN DAY CUBA

NAMES TO KNOW

The ousting of Gerardo Machado's regime in 1933 thrust Ramon Grau San Martin, a physiology professor at the University of Havana, and a cadre of students into authority. Grau implemented a range of forward-thinking policies that departed from Cuba's historical trajectory. However, the brief revolution of 1933 faltered.

Militarism's ascendancy, U.S. opposition, and internal rifts among Cuban political factions and within the revolutionary circles plunged the island back into tumultuous waters.

According to a *Cubans in America* article:

> Fulgencio Batista, an obscure army sergeant, emerged as the leader of the military after overthrowing the U.S.-trained officers and the Cuban officers. The military became the arbiter of Cuban politics. First through de facto ruling and finally with the popular election of Batista to the presidency in 1940. Batista collaborated with Grau in drafting the liberal Constitution of 1940, now without the Platt Amendment.

The conclusion of World War II and the demise of the initial Batista regime ushered in the successors of the 1933 revolution. In the democratic election of 1944, Grau San Martin ascended to the presidency, and four years later, his associate, Carlos Prio Socarras, assumed office, remaining in power until 1952. Following a period of residence in Florida, Batista returned to Cuba to run for president in 1952.

Facing certain electoral defeat, he led a military coup against President Carlos Prío Socarrás that preempted the election; however, Batista did win re-election to the presidency in the general election of 1954 and remained in office until December 31, 1958, when he was overthrown by revolutionary groups mostly lead by Fidel Castro.

On January 1, 1959, the toppling of dictator Batista signaled the dawn of a new era. Power lay in the streets, and Fidel Castro and his rebels came down from the mountains to claim it, and the rest, as they say, is history.

THE FABULOUS 50s

My dad would always tell me that in the 1950s, Havana was a magical place to live, work, and play. The Havana Hilton hotel, according to his memory, was the first hotel property in Cuba to install automatic sliding glass doors. Frank Sinatra and his Rat Pack entertained the locals and tourists at luxury casinos. In the 1950s, Havana was what today's Las Vegas is, except it had a beach and better weather! Of course, that all came crashing on January 1, 1959.

According to Natasha Geiling's article in *Smithsonian Magazine:*

> A 1956 issue of *Cabaret Quarterly,* a now-defunct tourism magazine, describes Havana as "a mistress of pleasure, the lush and opulent goddess of delights."
>
> By the 1950s Cuba was playing host to celebrities like Ava Gardner, Frank Sinatra and Ernest Hemingway. The cheap flights and hotel deals made the once-exclusive hotspot accessible to American masses. For around $50—a few hundred dollars today—tourists could purchase round-trip tickets from Miami, including hotel, food and entertainment. Big-name acts, beach resorts, bordellos and buffets were all within reach.
>
> "Havana was then what Las Vegas has become," says Louis Perez, a Cuba historian at the University of North Carolina at Chapel Hill. It attracted some of the same mafia kingpins, too, such as Meyer Lansky and Santo Trafficante, who were evading a national investigation into organized crime. […]
>
> By the late '50s, U.S. financial interests included 90 percent of Cuban mines, 80 percent of its public utilities, 50 percent of its railways, 40 percent of its sugar production and 25 percent of its bank deposits—some $1 billion in total. American influence extended into the cultural realm, as well. Cubans grew accustomed to the luxuries of American life. They drove American cars, owned TVs, watched Hollywood movies and shopped at Woolworth's department store. The youth listened to rock and roll, learned English in school, adopted American baseball and sported American fashions. (Geiling, 2007)

Cuba's proximity to Miami has always been the attraction. And will continue to be. I hope I am alive to see the day Cuba becomes a full fledge democracy.

THE BROMANCE: CUBA AND THE U.S.S.R.

For four decades Cuba became a close and faithful ally of the Soviet Union. In the 1970s, with Soviet support, Cuba sent several hundred thousand troops to Africa, intervened in Latin America, and supported revolutionary, anti-U.S. groups in the region. Cuba also became an ally of Iran and Syria and an enemy of Israel. Che Guevara attempted to spark revolutions in Africa and Bolivia, where he was killed. During the Yom Kippur Arab War against Israel in 1973, Cuba sent troops to support Syria. In the 1970s Cuban troops participated in the overthrow of the Somoza dynasty in Nicaragua. All this has been well documented.

The failure and collapse of the Soviet Union and Communism in Eastern Europe produced a major economic dislocation in Cuba and the beginning of "El Periodo Especial"—the "Special Period"—that included growing shortages of food, electricity, and transportation. There was mounting evidence of disillusionment with the Communist Party and Castro's exhortations. As a result, Castro was losing the battle to create a new generation devoted to anti-Americanism, the party, and the revolution.

CASTRO'S END (AGAIN) IS SOMEWHAT NEAR

In 2006, Castro fell ill and relinquished power. A quick and smooth succession to his brother, General Raul Castro followed. Little changed. Repression continued, the militarization of the economy increased, and Cubans continued to leave the island. Minor economic adjustments were implemented under Raul Castro, but Cuba was not moving toward a free market.

After a prolonged illness, Fidel Castro died on Friday night, November 25, 2016, the day after Thanksgiving. On November 26, 2016, I woke up to my iPhone's non-stop buzzing. My wife Mary Ann and I were in Palm Beach for the holiday weekend. I called my mother and shared the "good" news with her. While no one should be happy about another individual's death, it was different when it came to Fidel Castro. He, his brother, and his thugs have ruined thousands of lives, off and on the Island. He is responsible for the relocation of millions of Cubans, forced to leave their homeland.

When leaving Cuba, most Cubans had to leave everything they had. We certainly did when we left Cuba for Madrid, Spain.

*"Freedom is very expensive, and it's necessary to either resign yourself to live without it or decide to purchase it for what it's worth." – **José Martí***

Celebrating Castro's death in Little Havana, FL
(Photo Credit: Shutterstock)

Chapter 3

MIAMI NUANCES

The "Freedom" Tower in downtown, Miami. In the 1960s, the Federal Government process and document Cuban refugees at this site. For Cubans, this is our "Ellis Island."

DEMOCRATS VS. REPUBLICANS

I don't have any research, nor do I know if any exists, so this is an educated guess based on my own experience and in conversations with other Cubans. In the beginning, the Cubans who were eligible to vote, registered Democrat (1960s-1970s), probably because of Presidents Kennedy and Carter. In the 1980s and on, Cuban Americans registered Republicans; think President Ronald Reagan and Vice President George H.W. Bush, and their anti-communist stance.

President Kennedy:

As a community in the late 70s and 80s, we were still hurting from the failed Bay of Pigs invasion. A lot of Cubans blame President Kennedy for that failure. Had he authorized the second wave of air cover and provided more resources, who knows how that invasion would have ended? In the end, President Kennedy did buy back their freedom—those Cubans who were captured and imprisoned in Cuba during the invasion—but it was probably a case of "too little, too late."

President Carter:

Cuban Americans were unhappy that President Carter wanted to normalize relationships with Cuba. At the time, Carter could have given us his middle finger, and we would have taken that better than his philosophy and desires about the relationship between Cuba and the U.S.

President Reagan:

Cubans loved Reagan's tough anti-Castro and anti-communist stance. They fell deeply in love with him. And Reagan knew exactly what and when to say it. In his remarks at a rally in Miami, Reagan says that *"the Castro regime would not survive a Reagan administration."* MIC DROP!

Unfortunately, the regime did outlast Reagan's two terms. Let us recap: President John F. Kennedy doesn't authorize additional troops, firepower, or planes during the Bay of Pigs invasions. As a result, 1,400 Cuban exiles are captured and held in Cuba's worst prisons for a few years until a deal is cut for their release. A hundred or so die in the invasion.

Jimmy and Rosalynn Carter with Fidel Castro on March 30, 2011
(Photo Credit: Cubadebate/Reuters)

President Jimmy Carter begins to normalize relationships between Cuba and the U.S. At the same time, the Cuban American community is still in pain about the Bay of Pigs and Operation Peter Pan President Ronald Reagan, the great communicator, and running for President of the United States against President Carter, keeps his message to the Cuban community clear: CASTRO IS BAD. COMMUNISM IS BAD.

On May 20, 1983, President Reagan visited Little Havana's Esquina de Tejas restaurant and met with prominent Cuban Americans, including Jorge Mas Canosa. It was a historic day for the Cuban community, to have a sitting U.S. President celebrate Cuba's Independence from Spain.

THE MIAMI HERALD VS. THE CUBAN COMMUNITY

If you grew up in Miami between the 1970s and the 1990s, it's no secret that much of the Cuban American community disliked and distrusted our largest hometown newspaper, the Miami Herald. This rang so true that once I started working in Miami politics, where you learn by osmosis that media is not your friend; they are the enemy, and the *Miami Herald* is *enemigo numero uno!* At times it was challenging not engaging with the *Miami Herald* given my role as Executive Director of the Miami-Dade County Legislative Delegation.

I have also asked around and after hearing from various sources, including old timers, the Cuban community felt—putting it nicely—a lack of "fair and balanced" reporting by the Miami Herald of Cuban Americans that went back years. Even County Commissioner Jorge Valdez (Chapter 5) blamed the Miami Herald's coverage for his political demise (and timing) in 1990.

On January 18, 1992, the *Miami Herald* published an editorial against a congressional bill to tighten the U.S. embargo against Cuba. The Cuban American National Foundation (CANF)—a powerful group lead by businessman Jorge Mas Canosa—ardently supported the bill, believing it would help destroy Castro. The paper said it would hurt the Cuban people. On the same day, a columnist in *El Nuevo Herald* skewered unnamed "impostors, opportunists and gigolos who have made their modus vivendi out of anti-Castroism" (Bensch, Bragg; 1992). And it got really ugly and nasty, really quickly.

(Photo Credit: St. Petersburg Times/by Rick Brag, 1992.)

Later in this book, you will hear directly from David Lawrence, Jr., about his experience as the Publisher of the *Miami Herald* from 1989 to 1999. I encourage you to purchase David's book titled *A Dedicated Life: Journalism, Justice and a Chance for Every Child*. It is a fascinating read from someone who's had an incredible life and at 82 years young, keeps a busier calendar than most 40-year-olds.

Jorge Mas Canosa passed away on November 24, 1997. A brilliant businessman, he founded a Fortune 500 company, Mastec, as well as the CANF, the Cuban American National Foundation. Today, leading Mastec are his sons: Jose Mas serves as CEO and Jorge chairs the board.

In 1995, Alberto Ibargüen was named publisher of Knight Ridder's *El Nuevo Herald*, a Spanish language supplement whose audience was primarily Cuban Americans, and in 1998 he becomes publisher of the *Miami Herald*. He was the first Hispanic to that position. He served as publisher until 2005. By then things had settled down. Now two and half generations into this "exile," I am not sure that this is still the case—that Cubans hate the *Miami Herald*—nevertheless, it is another interesting nuance about Cuban Americans, our local newspaper and politics.

EXILES VS. IMMIGRANTS

According to the article "Cuban Exiles in America," of all the aspects of the Cuban Revolution, "none has had a greater impact on America than the immigration of over one million Cubans to the United States. Settling mostly in Miami, but also elsewhere, Cuban Americans have created a wealthy, successful, politically influential immigrant society" (PBS, 2005).

There were four waves of Cubans that came to the U.S. The first wave brought:

The Cubans who came to Miami in 1959 were supporters of the ousted Batista government. Soon they were joined by increasing numbers of wealthy Cubans whose property had been confiscated by the Cuban government: executives of U.S. companies and well-established professionals, including many doctors. Most did not expect exile to last long but thought Cuba would soon be liberated – first placing their hopes on the failed Bay of Pigs invasion, and later on the certainty that the United States would never allow the consolidation of a Communist government ninety miles away from their shores. (PBS, 2005)

The first wave (1959-1962), called "The Golden Exile," brought many successful business leaders including one that would go on to be the first Latino CEO of a Fortune 500 company: Robert Goizueta, who in March of 1981 was appointed CEO of the Coca-Cola Company, making American business history.

The second wave (1965-1973) is when we came to the U.S. from Spain. This was known as the "Freedom Flights" wave. This is when the "middle- and lower-middle classes, and skilled laborers" leave Cuba (or other countries to come to the U.S.). By 1974, an estimated 250,000 Cubans had entered the U.S.

We (my dad, my mom, and I) came to the U.S. in August of 1971 and immediately settled in Miami, Florida. We first lived in and around Little Havana, which today is a wonderful tourist destination. You should visit!

The third wave happened in 1980 during the Mariel Boat lift, which I write about later. The last wave (mid-1990s) is the "Balsero" or raft crisis, where many boat people ventured to Florida in homemade rafts and boats.

It is important to understand that Cuban Americans, certainly those who came in the first and second waves consider themselves "exiles" and not "immigrants." This is very important, and different from the later waves. Exile is commonly defined in the dictionary as someone who is "living in a foreign country because they cannot live in their own country, usually for political reasons." An immigrant is commonly defined as "a person who migrates to another country, usually for permanent residence."

Certainly, the first and second wave of Cubans thought of themselves as exiles. Cubans had high hopes that they would return to Cuba as soon as Fidel Castro's government failed. Something to consider, when individuals come to a country as an exile, versus an immigrant, these individuals are most likely educated, middle to upper class, had resources and lost what they owned because of a political take-over. And while they must "start over" in a new country, they use their knowledge, experience and education to start over, giving them a head start. That's not to say that immigrants can't make it. There are millions of immigrants who come to the U.S. with nothing and with hard work, luck, faith, and grit, become the classic "American Dream."

Generally speaking, and as defined, immigrants come to another country for a better life, may not have the educational attainment as that of exiles or other immigrants, and sometimes will send resources "back home" to take care of their families.

I hope that this little primer was helpful, providing some sort of understanding of the collective Cuban "mindset" which may explain how we act and behave, and why we've been successful in a relatively short amount of time. Of course, not everyone who is Cuban is a success story.

Chapter 4

THE TIES THAT BIND US

(Photo credit: LEILA MACOR/AFP via Getty Images)

To understand the rise of Cuban Americans in Florida politics and anywhere else, it is really important that you understand or have some context about what I call the "ties that bind us" as a community of exiles whose homeland sits 90 miles from the U.S. As I was writing this book, I thought deeply about those ties that most Cubans, regardless of where they are, their political leanings, wealth (or lack thereof), power and influence, and how long they've been in the U.S., would agree on. I thought about people like Carlos Mayans, who came to the U.S. from Cuba via the Pedro Pan program. Carlos served in the Kansas Legislature from 1993 to 2003. In April of 2003 he was elected mayor of Wichita, Kansas, and served one term.

Senator Bob Menendez (D-NJ), the son of Cuban exiles who grew up in a housing project, today serves as a United States senator. His son, Rob, was elected to the U.S. House of Representatives in 2022. A family legacy in the making.

Ted Cruz, United Stated Senator from the great state of Texas. Cruz's father, Rafael, fled Cuba after being tortured and imprisoned by the Castro regime. He settled in Texas with just $100 sewn into his underwear. A classic Cuban and American story. He got a job washing dishes making 50 cents an hour and learned English, later graduating from the University of Texas at Austin, with a degree in mathematics. Today, Rafael Cruz is a pastor in Dallas, and no doubt proud of his son.

Florida's own trailblazer Jeanette Nuñez, Florida's first Latina Lt. Governor. Jeanette served in the Florida legislature from 2010 to 2018, and as speaker pro tempore for her final two years in the office. Nuñez began her career as a Legislative Aide to then State Senator Alex Díaz de la Portilla. I have no doubt she will continue to blaze trails.

In this chapter, I focus on the six "ties" that have affected the lives of Cuban and Cuban Americans on and off the Island. To provide some context, I have written a bit about each situation, and I hope it is helpful.

They are:
- Bay of Pigs Invasion
- Pedro/Peter Pan Freedom flights
- 1980s Mariel Boatlift
- Brothers to the Rescue
- The Cuban Missile Crisis
- How the U.S. Embargo Became Law

BAY OF PIGS INVASION

Fidel Alejandro Castro Ruz took over as Prime Minister of Cuba on January 1, 1959. A Marxist-Leninist and Cuban nationalist, under Castro's regime, Cuba became a one-party communist state, where private industry and business were nationalized, and state socialist reforms were implemented throughout society. "Nationalize" is an interesting word. It means, "The process of transforming privately-owned assets into public assets by bringing them under the public ownership of a national government or state" (Merriam-Webster). Castro rejected democracy and instead sided with the USSR and allowed them to place nuclear weapons in Cuba, resulting in the Cuban Missile Crisis, a defining incident of the Cold War, in 1962.

Obviously, the United States would not allow nuclear weapons to be within 90 miles of its coastline. In response to Castro's alignment with the U.S.S.R., President Eisenhower allocated $13.1 million to the Central Intelligence Agency (CIA) in March 1960, for use against Castro. With the aid of Cuban counterrevolutionaries, the CIA proceeded to organize an invasion operation. As part of the CIA operation, Cuban exiles formed a military unit, Brigade 2506. The Brigade's purpose was to overthrow Castro and return Cuba to democracy.

Over 1,400 exiles were ready to return to Cuba and fight for freedom. Under the direction, of U.S. military personnel, the 1,400 volunteers trained in Guatemala. They were divided into five infantry battalions and one paratrooper battalion. On April 17, 1961, the group launched from Guatemala and Nicaragua by boat. Two days earlier, eight CIA-supplied B-26 bombers had attacked Cuban airfields and then returned to the U.S.

The main invasion force landed on the beaches of Playa Girón and Playa Larga in the Bay of Pigs, where it overwhelmed a local revolutionary militia. Initially, José Ramón Fernández led the Cuban Army counter-offensive; later, Castro himself took personal control, and eventually, 20,000 Cuban military soldiers fought in the invasion. As the Brigade fighters lost the strategic initiative, the international community found out about the invasion, and U.S. President John F. Kennedy decided to withhold further air support. This is key.

The plan devised during Eisenhower's presidency had required involvement of both air and naval forces. Without air support, the invasion was being conducted with only one-half of the forces that the CIA had deemed necessary. The exiles surrendered three days later on April 20. Most of the invading counter-revolutionary troops were publicly interrogated and put into Cuban prisons. About 114 died, some were able to escape, but the rest were captured by Castro's military regime. The invading force had been defeated within three days by the Cuban Revolutionary Armed Forces.

The invasion was a U.S. foreign policy failure. The invasion's defeat solidified Fidel Castro's role as a national hero and widened the political division between the two formerly allied countries. It pushed Cuba closer to the USSR. Those strengthened Soviet-Cuban relations would lead to the Cuban Missile Crisis in 1962, which would go on to define President Kennedy's term in office. For the next 20 months, the 1,100-1,200 exiles were imprisoned by the Castro regime in horrific conditions. Robert Kennedy, then U.S. Attorney General and President Kennedy's younger brother, struck a deal with Castro's regime: $53 million worth of baby food and medicine in exchange for the Cuban exiles.

On December 23, 1962, the first freed prisoners of the Brigade returned to the U.S. The rest would follow thereafter, and most stayed living in Miami, where they remained active in anti-Castro politics.

Most Cuban Americans who came in the 50s, 60s, and even 70s always assumed they would return to their beloved homeland as a democracy.

A young Julio Gonzalez-Rebull (Courtesy of the Gonzalez-Rebull Family)

President Kennedy and First Lady Jacqueline Kennedy came to the Miami Orange Bowl in December 1963 to welcome the prisoners of war from the Bay of Pigs who were liberated as a result of negotiations between the United States and Cuba. Mrs. Kennedy greeted the crowd in Spanish, showing support for the Cuban Americans in their own language.

I have had the privilege of knowing and working with a few of these incredible individuals, including former Florida State Representative Humberto Cortina, the first Bay of Pigs veteran elected to the Florida Legislature, my Principal at Miami-Private School, Mr. Alvarez, and Julio Gonzalez Rebull, who returned from the Invasion and had a wonderful and influential life in Miami as a political consultant and ad agency owner. I have tremendous affection and respect for him, and junior, his son.

President John & Mrs. Kennedy at the Miami Orange Bowl welcoming back 1,400 political prisoners who were part of the Bay of Pigs invasion

In 1980, President Reagan and First Lady Nancy Reagan came to place a floral arrangement beneath the Monument of the Eternal Flame of the soldiers and aviators who fought and died at the Bay of Pigs. This was a powerful moment for our community, cementing the Cubans' love for the Reagans. The monument is located in Little Havana, at the intersection of SW 8th Street and 13th Avenue.

The monument, which was dedicated on April 17, 1971, contains the names of the fallen (they are engraved on the monument) and there is an eternal flame at the top. It was reported that President Nixon "cabled his best wishes" for the occasion. Today, whenever I give out of town friends a tour of Miami, I always make a point to stop there.

During my first few years in Miami, we lived in or near Little Havana, and my uncle had a Phillips 66 gas station across from the monument. At that age, I did not understand the importance or significance of the monument. As I grew older, I learned more and more about how Cubans in Miami were trying to take back our beloved Cuba. The failure of the Bay of Pigs is very significant given the loss of life and the imprisonment of so many Cuban freedom fighters.

Cuban Americans leaders and Florida elected officials at the White House for a Bay of Pigs Ceremony. (Photo Courtesy of the Gonzalez-Rebull Family)

PEDRO PAN FREEDOM FLIGHTS

By 1960, Castro's regime began teaching school children military drills, how to bear arms, and anti-American songs. By the spring of 1960, the Cuban government announced the closing of secondary schools, and the opening of youth camps where Cuban school children would learn agricultural work. Communism at its finest, folks!

The "best students" would be sent on scholarships to study in the Soviet Union—what a prize! The other students in the sixth grade and up would have their school year canceled and go to work in the countryside. By 1961 the Cuban government would seize control of all private schools. Cuban parents began to fear the youth camps, closing of private schools, Cuban Literacy Campaign, and sending children to the Soviet Union; so, with little to no choices left, and not wanting their children to grow up in a communist society, thousands of Cuban parents felt their only way out was to send their children to the United States, alone by themselves.

I cannot begin to imagine the guilt and anguish those parents must have felt. And the possible psychological challenges it would create for the children who were sent to the U.S. alone, not knowing when they would see their parents again. The resiliency needed to survive this was extraordinary. But most of them felt God was on their side. In celebration of 2022 Hispanic Heritage Month, I posted on LinkedIn a story about Pedro Pan and wrote about their collective resiliency. It has received almost 13,000 impressions. I encourage you to read the post, and the comments.

THE CATHOLIC CHURCH TO THE RESCUE!

Father Bryan O. Walsh, director of the Catholic Welfare Bureau, developed Operation Peter Pan in November 1960. He was inspired by Pedro Menéndez, a fifteen-year-old Cuban boy who had immigrated to Miami to live with relatives who proved unable to provide for him and sought assistance from the Catholic Welfare Bureau. Walsh understood that many similar youngsters would follow Pedro's steps to the United States as Fidel Castro established a Communist government. Speculation that this new government was planning to send minors to the Soviet Union to serve in work camps was causing panic in Cuban families who could not afford to escape.

Walsh contacted Tracy Voorhees, a veteran U.S. government official who was serving as the president's Personal Representative for Cuban Refugees, who suggested the Eisenhower Administration could provide funds to support Cuban immigrants once they reached Miami. James Baker, the headmaster of an American school in Havana, met with Walsh and detailed his efforts helping parents expatriate their children to Miami. Before meeting Walsh, Baker's original goal was to establish a boarding school in the United States for Cuban refugee children. However, both later agreed professional social welfare agencies would be better equipped to care for the children.

Operation Peter Pan was formed with the understanding that Baker would arrange the children's transportation, and Walsh would arrange for accommodations in Miami. Baker would facilitate the transportation via student visas issued by the American Embassy in Havana. Underground organizations led by the involved parents spread information regarding Operation Peter Pan. Among those who helped alert parents about the program were Penny Powers, Pancho and Bertha Finlay, Drs. Sergio and Serafina Giquel, Sara del Toro de Odio, and Albertina O'Farril. To maintain confidentiality, the program's leaders in the U.S. minimized their communications with their contacts in Cuba.

Between December 26, 1960, and October 23, 1962, it is estimated that 14,000 Cuban kids were sent to Miami without their parents. Operation Peter Pan ended when all air traffic between the United States and Cuba ceased in the aftermath of the Cuban Missile Crisis of October 1962.

Cuban immigrants needed to travel via Spain or Mexico to reach the United States until December 1965 when the United States established a program of Freedom Flights to unite Cuban parents with their children. The Catholic Welfare Bureau reported that once the Freedom Flights began nearly 90% of the minors still in its care were reunited with their parents. The program was unknown outside of Miami until the *Cleveland Plain Dealer* detailed its size and procedures.

Barry University, my alma mater, probably has the most comprehensive documents and stories on Pedro Pan, housed as part of the University's Archives and Special Collections and the *"Living Legacy Exhibit,"* both are located at Barry University's main campus at 11300 NE 2nd Avenue, Miami Shores, Florida 33161.

1980s MARIEL BOATLIFT

The Mariel Boatlift: 125,000 Cubans Come to America. The year was 1980 and Jimmy Carter was President of the United States and seeking re-election. President Carter was friendly to the Cuban Regime; his Administration had lifted all restrictions on travel to Cuba, and in September 1977, both countries established an Interest Section in each other's capital—just short of reopening embassies.

It wasn't all roses. Relations were strained because Cuba sent troops to support the Soviet Union's military interventions in Africa and the Middle East. The two countries struggled to reach agreement on a relaxation of the U.S. embargo on trade to permit the importation of a select list of medicines to Cuba without provoking Carter's political opponents in the U.S. Congress.

Ten members of Congress visited Cuba in December 1978, and the Cuban government later released the U.S. manager of a business in Cuba who had been prevented from leaving in 1963, accused of being a CIA agent, and sentenced to 50 years in prison.

A group of 55 people whose parents brought them from Cuba returned for three weeks in December 1978 in a rare instance of Cuba allowing the return of Cuban-born exiles.

In December 1978, both countries agreed upon their maritime border, and the next month, they were working on an agreement to improve their communications in the Straits of Florida. The U.S. responded to Cuban relaxation of restrictions on emigration by allowing Cuban Americans to send up to $500 to an emigrating relative (equivalent to $2,000 in 2020 dollars).

In November 1978, Castro's government met in Havana with a group of Cubans living in exile, agreed to grant an amnesty to 3,600 political prisoners, and announced that they would be freed in the course of the next year and allowed to leave Cuba. By May 1979, tours were being organized for Americans to participate in the Cuban Festival of Arts (Carifesta) in July, with flights departing from Tampa, Mexico City, and Montreal.

FAST FORWARD TWELVE MONTHS

The Mariel boatlift was a mass emigration of Cubans, who traveled from Cuba's Mariel Harbor, hence the name, to the United States between April 15 and October 31, 1980. Hundreds of Cuban Americans in Miami either chartered boats, yachts, or used their own to bring relatives back to Miami. It is estimated that 1,600 vessels were involved in the Mariel Boatlift. For those months, TV coverage in Miami was about the flotilla of boats heading to Cuba.

The term "Marielito" (plural "Marielitos") is used to refer to these refugees in both Spanish and English. The term is not meant to be nice or a compliment. While the exodus was triggered by a sharp downturn in the Cuban economy, it followed on the heels of generations of Cubans who had come to the United States in the preceding decades to search for political freedom and, later, for economic opportunities.

After 10,000 Cubans tried to gain asylum by taking refuge on the grounds of the Peruvian embassy, the Cuban government announced that anyone who wanted to leave could do so. The ensuing mass migration was organized by Cuban Americans, with the agreement of Cuban President Fidel Castro.

The arrival of the refugees in the United States created political problems for President Carter, as his Administration struggled to develop a consistent response, and many of the refugees had been released from jails and mental health facilities in Cuba. It was a brilliant move on Castro's part, empty his "basket of deplorables"—convicts, murderers, mentally unstable—and send them to the U.S., mixed in with others. In the end, according to a *Miami Herald* analysis, only 3% of the Marielitos fell into that category.

The movie Scarface is the fictional story of Antonio "Tony" Montana, a Marielito who once allowed to stay in the U.S. becomes one of the biggest drug dealers in Florida. If you have not seen the movie, I encourage you to do so. First, it is a classic. Second, you'll see Miami as it was before South Beach became famous, and third, Al Pacino and the cast are incredible in the movie.

Of course, not every Cuban agrees with me. Quite the opposite. The Cuban exile community at the time was outraged by the film because of its portrayal of Cubans, and rightly so, as it did not paint us in a good light. First, several of the main characters in the film were played by non-Cubans. Second, it portrayed a group of Cubans who were already not seen in a good light, as the new drug kings. Lastly, it should have been obvious that a film portraying Cuban immigrants as violent, drug-addicted mafioso types would not be well received by the community it was negatively stereotyping. Think *The Godfather* and how Italian Americans were portrayed, and their fight to kill production of the film, you get the picture—pun intended. Miami's Cuban community spoke loudly enough that production of the film was moved from Miami to Los Angeles.

The Mariel boatlift was ended by mutual agreement between the two governments in late October 1980. By then, as many as 125,000 Cubans had reached Florida.

A boat arrives in with Cuban refugees from Mariel Harbor, circa April 1980.
(Photo by Tim Chapman/Miami Herald)

THE MARIEL BOAT LIFT AND GOVERNOR BILL CLINTON'S 1980 RE-ELECTION LOSS

According to the Clinton House Museum:

President Jimmy Carter notified Clinton that Fort Chaffee, in northwest Arkansas, was to be a stop-over point for almost 20,000 Cuban refugees who had sought asylum in the U.S. along with 100,000 others. Rumor had it that the Freedom Flotilla contained refugees who were criminals and mentally ill.

Clinton publicly supported Carter's decisions. "I know that everyone in this state sympathizes and identifies with them in their desire for freedom. I will do all I can to fulfill whatever responsibilities the President imposes upon Arkansas to facilitate the refugees resettlement in this country."

[...] By late May, the camp's population had grown tremendously, and tensions began to mount both inside and outside its walls. Residents rushed to gun shops to protect themselves.

On May 26, 1980, one day before the primary election, up to 300 refugees turned over barricades and escaped through an unguarded gate, dispersing throughout the county. The federal troops stationed there did nothing about it. Within days, state troopers and local police recaptured the refugees with no help at all from the federal officers.

On the night of June 1, Fort Chaffee exploded as the refugees rioted. The press called it "a war zone". About 1,000 angry refugees charged the gate, and federal troops did nothing to stop them. About 200 refugees ran down Highway 22 in the direction of Barling, a small town near Fort Smith. At the end of the night, 62 people suffered injuries, including five refugees, who were shot.

Things settled down for a little bit until August when President Carter ordered the remaining 10,000 refugees to be sent to Fort Chaffee. Governor Clinton turned down the President's request, but the White House overruled the Governor. The people of Arkansas were angry.

Frank White, Clinton's GOP opponent had a slogan that would win him a spot in the Governor's Mansion: "Cubans and Car Tags." White criticized Clinton for his automobile tax increase, for not standing up to President Carter during the Cuban refugee crisis, and for not recruiting enough companies or stimulating sufficient job growth. [...]

On election night in 1980, the 34-year-old Clinton conceded to White. [...] No Arkansas governor since 1954 had been defeated for a second term. This race was a stunning upset in Arkansas political history [...]. Clinton later recalled that his loss to Frank White was the most painful experience he had ever gone through. ("1980", 2024)

BROTHERS TO THE RESCUE

On February 24, 1996, the Cuban Air Force shot two Brothers to the Rescue planes down in international airspace.

It has been over 25 years since this disgusting incident took place, and I still cannot believe it happened and that we, the U.S., did not retaliate as we should have. It's pure bullshit!

Brothers to the Rescue, or *Hermanos al Rescate*, as it's known in Spanish/Cuban speak is a Miami-based nonprofit organization headed by José Basulto and formed by Cuban exiles. The group is widely known for its opposition to the Cuban government and its former leader Fidel

Castro. The group describes itself as a humanitarian organization aiming to assist and rescue raft refugees emigrating from Cuba and to "support the efforts of the Cuban people to free themselves from dictatorship through the use of active non-violence."

The organization was founded in May 1991 "after several pilots were touched by the death of fifteen-year-old Gregorio Perez Ricard who fleeing Castro's Cuba on a raft, perished of severe dehydration in the hands of U.S. Coast Guard officers who were attempting to save his life." The Cuban government accused them of involvement in terrorist acts and infiltrated the group.

In their official transcripts, the Cuban pilots boasted about destroying the "cojones" of their victims. The incident was condemned internationally, including by the UN Security Council, while the Cuban government defended the decision claiming the planes were there to destabilize the Cuban government. The Castro-approved mission against Brothers to the Rescue was codenamed "Operation Scorpion."

At the time, U.S. Secretary of State Madeleine Albright immediately denounced the murders, saying, "This is not cojones, it is cowardice." She also wore her blue bird pin with its head pointing down, in mourning for the four Cuban-American fliers killed in the tragedy.

A blue bird pin reinforced Secretary of State Albright's approach to sending messages with her jewelry. She also wore her blue bird pin with its head pointing down, in mourning for the four Cuban-American fliers killed in the tragedy.

THE CUBAN MISSILE CRISIS

It is well known that in October of 1962, the U.S.S.R. wanted to install nuclear-armed Soviet missiles in Cuba, which is about 90 miles away from Key West, Florida.

According to the Department of State's Office of the Historian, President Kennedy on national television to inform Americans of the situation, saying, "It shall be the policy of this nation to regard any nuclear missile launched from Cuba against any nation in the Western Hemisphere as an attack by the Soviet Union on the United States, requiring a full retaliatory response upon the Soviet Union."

Following this news, many people feared the world was on the brink of nuclear war. However, disaster was avoided when Soviet leader Nikita Khrushchev offered to remove the Cuban missiles in exchange for the U.S. promising not to invade Cuba. Kennedy also secretly agreed to remove U.S. missiles from Turkey. (History. com Editors, 2023)

I know this was a very brief primer on the Cuban Missile Crisis. It definitely deserves more. There are plenty of books on this, and I would encourage you to seek them out because it was a defining moment between the U.S. and the U.S.S.R., which stood for the Union of Soviet Socialist Republics.

HOW THE U.S. EMBARGO BECAME LAW

The U.S. first imposed an embargo on the sale of arms to Cuba on March 14, 1958, during the Fulgencio Batista regime. Again, on October 19, 1960, the U.S. placed an embargo on exports to Cuba except for food and medicine after Cuba nationalized American-owned Cuban oil refineries without compensation. On February 7, 1962, the embargo was extended to include almost all exports. The embargo does not prohibit the trade of food and humanitarian supplies.

As of 2018, the Cuban embargo is enforced mainly through six statutes:

i. The Trading with the Enemy Act of 1917
ii. The Foreign Assistance Act of 1961
iii. The Cuban Assets Control Regulations of 1963
iv. The Cuban Democracy Act of 1992
v. Helms-Burton Act of 1996
vi. The Trade Sanctions Reform and Export Enhancement Act of 2000

The stated purpose of the Cuban Democracy Act of 1992 is to "maintain sanctions on Cuba if the Cuban government refuses to move toward "democratization and greater respect for human rights." The Helms-Burton Act further restricted United States citizens from doing business in or with Cuba, and mandated restrictions on giving public or private assistance to any successor government in Havana unless and until certain claims against the Cuban government were met.

In 1999 President Bill Clinton expanded the trade embargo by disallowing U.S. companies' foreign subsidiaries to trade with Cuba. In 2000 Clinton authorized the sale of food and "humanitarian" products to Cuba. In Cuba, the embargo is called el bloqueo (the blockade), despite there being no naval blockade of the country by the United States since the Cuban Missile Crisis in 1962. The Cuban government frequently blames the US "blockade" for the economic problems of Cuba.

SO HOW DID THIS EMBARGO BECOME LAW?

"I've been Rolled." Were the exact words that U.S. Senator Chris Dodd (D-CT) said once he realized that the Helms-Burton legislation that President Clinton's team had agreed to after days of negotiation included codification.

I feel *so* privileged to have had an opportunity to interview my friend, mentor, and former Congressman Lincoln Díaz-Balart (LDB), for this section. He is one of the most amazing public servants I've ever met. LDB provided me—and now you—with a behind the scenes, firsthand account of what it took to get the embargo codified into law. And he should know, he was there, he was a driving force. Below is his story, in his own words.

While we waited for Senator Helms to be summoned so we could speak to the press and publicly announce the deal, something happened which was personally memorable for me. We were in the large conference room next to the Senate International Relations Chairman's inner office, when Senator Christopher Dodd poked his head in the room. I smiled at him with a look of deep satisfaction and success. He said, "I've been rolled," and left.

That moment was memorable for me because only Ronald Reagan was more responsible for my leaving the Democratic Party in 1985 than Christopher Dodd. [...] When President Reagan was trying to prevent a communist takeover of Central America, Christopher Dodd had become the "foreign policy face" of the Democratic Party.

He and the Democratic Leadership in Congress during the 1980s did everything they could to derail Ronald Reagan's fight for freedom in Central America. Christopher Dodd also did all he could to help the Castro dictatorship. He and Congressman Charles Rangel of New York were the most zealous and effective defenders of the Castro dictatorship's interests in the U.S. Congress until the arrival of Congressman (later Senator) Jeff Flake of Arizona in 2001. Dodd's acknowledgement that we had "rolled" him in 1996, was, indeed, memorable.

Later, the Clinton team met to review the agreement. When the State and Defense Secretaries and the Attorney General heard about codification, they objected. But Clinton's political advisors, George Stephanopoulos and Leon Panetta, overruled them.

They knew Dole could be defeated in 1996. But Americans had been killed, and it was not a good idea for Clinton to give Dole an issue. So, the Clinton advisors focused on their Title III "win," which they would use to explain their change of position on Helms-Burton. And Clinton stated he would sign the bill.

We passed it by a final vote of 74 to 22 in the Senate on March 5, and 336 to 86 in the House on March 6. Clinton signed it in the Old Executive Office Building of the White House on March 12, 1996.

The embargo was now U.S. law. It could not be lifted – by Clinton, nor later by Obama – because the law requires the President of the United States to certify to Congress that a transitional government is in power in Cuba. In other words, that very important conditions have been met.

Those conditions include the release of all political prisoners in Cuba; the legalization of all political activity including independent political parties, free labor unions and the press; and the scheduling of internationally supervised elections. Section 102 (h) states:

Codification of Economic Embargo – The economic embargo of Cuba, as in effect on March 1, 1996, including all restrictions under part 515 of title 31, Code of Federal Regulations, shall be in effect upon the enactment of this Act, and shall remain in effect, subject to section 204 of this Act.

Helms-Burton's codification transferred the essence of U.S. policy toward Cuba from the President to Congress. Bill Clinton and Barack Obama (even with a majority in both Houses of Congress for the first two years of his presidency) were not able to lift the embargo.

Photo of Rafael Díaz-Balart with his four sons: Rafael, Lincoln, Jose and Mario

Chapter 5
MIAMI:
1960S – 2000S

"FUN IN THE SUN" TO "COCAINE COWBOYS"

Those are some of the headlines that Miami has laid claim to. To understand the rise of Cuban Americans in politics in Florida, you need to understand *how* Cubans transformed Miami from an annual winter and Spring Break vacation destination to the international, sexy, world class city it is today.

The 1960s defined Miami as the "Sun and Fun Capital of the World," thanks to Jackie Gleason's weekly television show. That probably inspired the "Greatest Generation" to flock to Miami and Miami Beach in the 1970s and 1980s and retire, enjoying sunny days almost all year long.

In 1972, Miami Beach was home to both the Democratic National and the Republican National conventions. Both were televised, showing the hostile crowds. Politically speaking, it was a turbulent time in our country, and this was reflected at both conventions.

When my family moved to West Miami in 1973 – my parents purchased their home, cementing the American Dream – we were the only "Cubans" in the neighborhood. There was not much building further west than State Road 826, aka, the Palmetto Highway and maybe 87th Avenue?

Side Bar: if you really want to see the "South Beach" that I grew up with, get *The Last Resort* and you will see what it was really like.

You can also watch the first few minutes of the movie *Scarface* starring Al Pacino. There are some great scenes of South Beach. But be warned, the chainsaw scene is pretty gruesome.

SHOULD WE STAY? OR SHOULD WE GO?

There was another shift happening: a mindset shift about whether Cubans (mostly the older ones) would go back to Cuba or begin a new life in the U.S. There were never any discussions in my household or in my immediate family's about going back. My personal opinion is that any hope of going back to Cuba was finally dashed in 1980 with the Mariel Boatlift. At that point, there was a collective realization that the U.S. was our new home and, therefore, we would fully embrace "The American Dream" and adopt and adapt to our new homeland.

Some historians would describe the early 1980s in Miami as terrible years. The November 23, 1981 issue of *Time* magazine features a map of the state of Florida with the words "Paradise Lost" across it, with an unhappy sun.

Miami, Fort Lauderdale, and West Palm Beach made the FBI's annual list of the ten most crime-ridden cities in the nation. In 1980, Miami had the nation's highest murder rate and an estimated 70% of all marijuana and cocaine imported into the U.S. passed through South Florida. It definitely was bad, but as we all know, it is during the worst of times that hope shines brightest.

A SHIFTING DEMO AND THE 1992 REAPPORTIONMENT

Every 10 years the United States government does a count called the U.S. Census. The government needs to know how many people live in the U.S., where they live, how many people live together, or by themselves, etc. Once the government has collected all that information, each state must redraw congressional seats to ensure that each Congressional district has roughly the same number of residents. This also applies to the state senate and state representative districts, and to local districts as well. Think of it as a re-balancing act.

The states with the largest population will have the largest number of congressional districts, i.e., largest number of seats in Congress. As states lose population, they also lose representation in Congress, with the exception of U.S. Senators, those stay the same: two per state, regardless of size, loss or gain of population. At the state level, the districts usually increase in population, becoming more compact. In Florida for example, for every three (3) state representative districts, there is one (1) state senate district. This is how we get 120 districts in the House and 40 in the Senate.

In 1982, after the redistricting process, three Cuban Americans were elected to the Florida House of Representatives and by 1989, during a special Congressional election, Ileana Ros-Lehtinen (IRL) was elected to Congress, making *"herstory"* by becoming the first Hispanic/Latina woman to serve in the United States Congress.

By 1990, there were 12 Cuban Americans in the Florida Legislature: three (3) in the Senate and nine (9) in the House. By 2000, almost two dozen Cuban Americans had served in the Florida legislature and two were serving in Congress. By the 2000s Census, Miami-Dade County's population was at 2,253,362 people, with Hispanics comprising 57% or 1,291,737 million people.

In conversations with my friend Alex Penelas, he reminded me that in addition to the reapportionment process, Hurricane Andrew played a significant role in changing the demographics of South Dade. Hurricane Andrew, which made landfall on August 24, 1992, just a few weeks prior to a statewide primary election, was the costliest hurricane on record at the time, $27B worth of damage, $55B in today's economy. Over 100,000 homes were wiped out, 250,000 people were left homeless, 82,000 businesses were destroyed, 1.4 million people lost power at the height of the storm; some for more than one month, and South Dade lost over 100,000 residents. They never came back. As the rebuilding efforts began, those 100,000, mostly Anglo residents, were replaced by Hispanic families, thus causing a large demographic shift in South Dade never seen before. Today, according to the 2020 Census, Hispanics comprised 65% of the population.

As you may imagine, the demographic shift, which was happening fast, did not settle well with some. Miami was becoming more international as a city. It was cementing its title as the "Gateway to Latin America," definitely becoming more and more Cuban.

As a result, it was not unusual to see t-shirts and bumper stickers that read: "Will the last American to leave Miami please bring the flag."

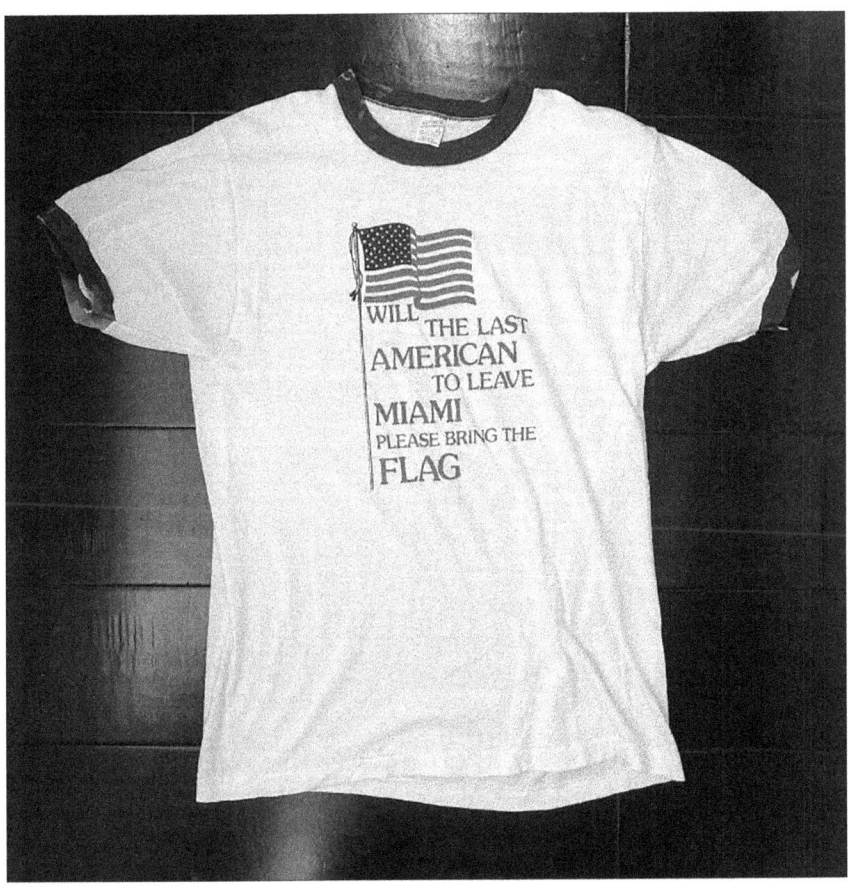

(Photo Credit: Miami Herald)

Chapter 6

STUMBLING INTO HISTORY

My introduction to politics was purely by accident. At the time, summer of 1988, I was attending Miami-Dade College (MDC), then Miami-Dade Community College. It was my fourth year at MDC—a two-year degree institution—and I had reached a point of no return. It finally hit me that I would never be an architect. I could never comprehend the math that was required: algebra, trigonometry, calculus; I have needed a math tutor since I was in second or third grade. Who was I kidding?

I was disappointed, depressed, distraught, and burned out. I felt lost not knowing what to do next because since I was eight years old, all I wanted to be was an architect and design beach houses in Florida.

A high school friend, Maytee Sanz, was working in the office of Florida State Senator Ileana Ros-Lehtinen. She had been with her for a few years and wanted to experience Tallahassee, FL, and the legislative session. Maytee convinced Ileana to send her to Tallahassee as long as she would have a staff person replace her in Miami. That is where I came into the picture. Stumbling into politics, but really into political history.

I learned a lot that summer working for her, spending time with her, her parents, Amanda and Enrique Ros, and just watching and observing her. Everybody loved, adored, and respected her.

When you start out working for someone like IRL—that's what the staff call her—you have a responsibility to be your best. She is providing you with the opportunity to represent her brand, so you need to be top of your game because that is what people expect, not to mention that by working with her, opportunities will come your way, no doubt about it. Looking back on it now, I am so glad I started working with IRL. She really set the bar high, and that's exactly what you need when you are young and impressionable. It was what I needed.

MY FIRST CAMPAIGNS

After the internship with Ileana, I met a smart, young, political consultant named Alex Díaz—today he goes by Díaz de la Portilla—who was the campaign manager for Shaun Herness' campaign. Herness was running for State Representative District 114.

Alex was very charming, smooth, drove a baby blue convertible BMW and dressed like Richard Gere in *American Gigolo*. A year older than me, yet so much savvier, extremely likeable, and one hell of a smooth operator. Directly from central casting, as they say in Hollywood, California.

Shaun had worked for State Representative Javier Souto as a legislative aide and decided to run for office. It was a Republican primary, and the opponent was Bruce Hoffman, a lawyer. We lost that race to Bruce, who once in office, would end up hiring my best friend of many years, Alex J. Fernandez. Bruce's wife, Marion, and I are great friends and someone I admire tremendously. That is the "small world" of politics and the political process.

Alex Díaz and I stayed friends and in contact after the campaign. With my Herness campaign and internship experiences, I thought I was a political wunderkind, ready for my next challenge. More on Alex and his family is featured in the book.

For me, the next stop was another campaign. This one was a state-wide campaign called "Amendment 10" which pitted the trial lawyers against the doctors and centered on medical malpractice caps. Doctors wanted to cap damages at $250,000. Trial lawyers opposed caps.

This is where I met Marian P. Bailey, now Johnson. Marian ran the trial lawyer's political action committee and was the campaign manager for the Amendment 10 campaign. It did not dawn on me what a trailblazer and ceiling breaker she was—still is—and how much I would learn from her. Here we are in 1988 and a woman is running a statewide campaign in Florida. Working for trial lawyers who are mostly white males, she was in charge. WOW!

While at Amendment 10, I had the opportunity to meet some of the state's most powerful and influential trial lawyers, people like Wayne Hogan, Karen Gievers, John Romano, A.J. Cone and a Cuban American lawyer from the Orlando area named Mel Martinez, who would go on to serve as a United States Senator from Florida and Secretary of Housing under George W. Bush's presidency. A Pedro Pan, he has a remarkable story. I encourage you to read up on him.

These are the kind of trial lawyers that get verdicts in the millions of dollars. These are life-changing for their clients, some of whom need 24-hour medical care as a result of their injuries. It was nice to work with them and hear their war stories. As the campaign was wrapping up, Marian offered me a job in Tallahassee. I told her I wasn't ready yet, but if I decided to move to Tally, I would let her know. She said I would always have a job on her team, even if she had to create one.

TALLAHASSEE, HERE I COME!

After the Amendment 10 campaign, which we won, I held several menial jobs, and was hoping to get back into politics. As luck would have it, a newly elected member of the Florida House, Nilo Juri (R-Hialeah), was looking for a legislative aide that could travel to Tallahassee for the 1989 legislative session. After what seemed like a very long interview, and a phone call from Ileana Ros-Lehtinen a few days later, Nilo Juri offered me the job. I was so excited to be a legislative aide and travel to Tallahassee for the Legislative session.

One of my favorite sayings is by Roman philosopher Seneca, "Luck is what happens when preparation meets opportunity." In life, I have found it really helpful to be prepared, to know your subject matter, know how you are working with or speaking too. Do your research on what is being discussed. It is equally important to know what you want. What kind of job? What kind of individual do you want to work for or with? How much money would you like to make?

I am a strong believer that opportunities will always be around; however, if you are not prepared and don't know what you want, you will miss them. They will be unrecognizable to you, and that's a shame.

As a result of the deal the Cuban legislators made with Tom Gustafson, basically securing his election as Speaker of the Florida House in 1988, Nilo Juri's legislative aide, Jose Fuentes, was promoted to run the Cuban American Caucus Office in Tallahassee, creating an opportunity for me to "replace" him.

Being the first director of the Cuban America Caucus office opened many doors for Jose, and as a result, today he is a very successful government affairs executive at Becker, one of Florida's most prominent law firms.

After 35 years since first meeting Jose, we are still friends, have supported each other over the years, and it is a wonderful example of what I have termed "the beauty of politics."

The same "luck" that Jose provided to me, I provided to a young, smart, and very politically savvy 19-year-old named Ana Carbonell, who "replaced" me when I left Nilo's office.

Ana's mom was Nilo's travel agent, and she would always talk to me about her daughter and how Ana loved politics and would love to work with an elected official. So, when I was getting ready to leave Nilo's office, I shared the news with Edita (Edith) and we began plotting on how to hire Ana. I figured Nilo, with me gone, would be caught in a tight spot, and him knowing Edita, he would hire Ana, which is exactly what happened, and the rest, as they say, is history.

Ana would go on to work for State Senator Lincoln Díaz-Balart, then Congressman Lincoln Díaz-Balart, eventually become his Chief of Staff—at 25 years of age—probably one of the first and youngest Latinas to hold that role in the United States Congress. Today, she runs a very successful political firm advising Unites States Senators, Governors, and Presidential candidates, amongst others.

THE FLORIDA HOUSE OF REPRESENTATIVES

In the House, as a legislative aide, I worked with State Representatives like Rudy Garcia, Luis Morse, Willie Logan, Jimmy Burke, Beryl Burke, Elaine Bloom, Mike Abrams, John Cosgrove, Alberto Gutman, Larcenia Bullard, Elaine Gordon, the Díaz-Balart brothers—in fact Nilo was their roommate during the 1989 session. I was there when history was being made. It is the equivalent of today's "being in the room where it happens," all this at the age of 22 to 25.

In April of 1989, I packed my red Toyota Celica and headed to Tallahassee for the legislative session. The first weeks were a bit awkward as it was a new environment, new people, new setting. It was also the first time I would be on my own, away from friends, family, and the comforts of home.

At heart, I am an introvert, always have been and always will be, so I was really pushing myself out of my comfort zone. As the session progressed, I was having the time of my life, making new friends, meeting other legislative aides, elected officials, and learning the legislative process. I also met some really great young political operatives who have become lifelong friends.

St. Augustine, FL, weekend road trip circa early 1990s. L-R: Gene Wilk, Me, David Custin, Joe Fraga, and Omar Franco. (Photo courtesy of Carlos F. Orta)

During this time in politics, Republicans and Democrats tended to work together, especially those from Miami, really South Florida. The staff also worked together—political party nor race, nor religion mattered. The only rule we had was not to talk badly about each other's bosses. You could speak ill of your boss, but not theirs. Simple, but effective.

Those 60 days in Tallahassee, you learn so much about yourself and the political process. It was my first session, and I had no clue what I was doing. Nilo was obsessed about Hialeah politics, and it was his first session too, so it was interesting learning from each other.

In the late 1980s, the Sergeant-at-Arms for the House of Representatives would produce a weekly calendar/schedule type booklet. On the cover of the book was the schedule for the week, detailing when the various House committees COULD meet that week. When one of Nilo's committees was listed on the front cover of the calendar, I would send him to the appropriate meeting room. A few minutes later, he would come back and tell me no one was there. There was no committee meeting. I did not understand why. The committee was listed on the cover. Why would it not meet?

After sending him to three committee meetings that WERE NOT MEETING, Nilo, naturally very frustrated with me, sent me to the House Governmental Operations Committee, where he was Vice-Chair. He told the Committee Staff Director to explain to me the legislative process, what happens during session, when committees are meeting, etc. I would go off to the Gov Opps committee for my tutoring lessons twice, sometimes three times a week. By the time the session finished, I knew as much as someone who had gone through several sessions. It was a smart move on Nilo's part, and I am so grateful he did that for me.

I finally figured out that just because the committee was listed on the front cover of the schedule, that did not mean it was actually scheduled to meet. To know for sure if there was a committee meeting, you had to open up the booklet, go to the day (and time) it was scheduled to meet and see if it was listed on that day. I am surprised Nilo did not fire me that session!

I can tell you that being a legislative aide was hard work, long hours, especially as the session got closer to the end. We did not have google or the internet, cell phones were boxy and very expensive.

Every day you would have dozens of people stop by your office to speak to your boss. This could be a group of Miamians who came to Tally to lobby for a bill, a group of kids from Orlando who wanted to preserve a state park, or a group of judges who lobbied for the judicial system and its annual appropriations. The crowds mostly depended on the committees your boss served on, but not always.

Working in a challenging environment taught me how to handle all kinds of individuals and personalities. The majority of constituents were very nice. A small minority were not so nice. Sometimes just plain rude. It also taught me how to prioritize issues and conversations. How to work with other staffers from around the state who either fawned over the fact that I was from Miami or did not like the fact that I was from Miami. Remember, this is over 30 years ago. I was surprised by how many elected and appointed officials from around the rest of the state, and their staff had never visited Miami or South Florida.

I also met some interesting people, some famous people, sports icons, and of course other politicians. I had the opportunity to spend half a day with Gloria and Emilio Estefan when they visited Tallahassee to lobby for boat safety legislation. Julius "Dr. J" Ervin, who at the time owned a Coca-Cola franchise, if I remember right, was lobbying for some business issue I cannot recall. While you were in Tallahassee, you also had to keep tabs on what was going on in the district office, and with those constituents. It was constant chaos for 60 days.

In 1990, I returned to Tallahassee with a new State Representative, Miguel De Grandy, a trial lawyer. He was impressed by my knowledge of the process, the shortcuts you could take, and all the committee staffers and legislative personnel I knew. It made me feel good that someone as smart as Miguel was impressed by me. During those first years, being around so many smart, sharp, quick-witted people, I use to question my intellect/smarts. Not having a college degree made it worse for me, and I was very self-conscious.

Miguel is one of the smartest, if not the smartest person, for whom I have ever worked. His brain was built for law and politics, and his heart for taking care of those who cannot take care of themselves.

The perfect public servant. After two legislative sessions (1989 and 1990), I decided to move to Tallahassee to continue working in politics and returned to community college to earn that elusive Associate of Arts (AA) degree. I called my former boss, Marian P. Bailey, and told her about my plans. Keeping true to her promise, she hired me at the Florida Lawyers Action Group (FLAG), the political action committee of the Academy of Florida Trial Lawyers, one of the most influential special interest groups in Tallahassee.

I spent the summers of 1991 and 1992 in Tallahassee at FLAG, learning from Marian and her 30+ years of experience in Florida politics. She is the "Google" of Florida politics.

At some point in 1992, things went south with Marian and the Academy of Florida Trial Lawyers. She left and joined their arch enemy, the Associated Industries of Florida. The Academy's executive director, Scott Carruthers, was not very nice to me once Marian was gone, so I too knew my days were numbered. In fact, the day after Marian left, Scott had the office door re-keyed and locked me out of my computer so that I could not access any information. I came to learn this is standard operating procedure (SOP).

With the help of Miguel De Grandy, Scott relocated me to Miami, where I was assigned to work full-time for the campaign of a young trial lawyer the Academy was backing named Alex Villalobos.

Back then, early 1980s and 1990s, as a Cuban American, if you were going to run for office in Miami, it helped to run as a Republican, be good looking, young, lawyer, and come from a family of politicians or business leaders who opposed the Castro regime in Cuba and fled to Miami seeking exile. Alex checked all the boxes. His grandfather, Lolo Villalobos, at the age of 20 in 1933, while attending the University of Havana Medical School, became the chief of the Havana Aqueduct. In 1940, at the age of 27, Lolo Villalobos was elected as Mayor of the City of Guanabacoa and was re-elected six consecutive times. In January 1959, after Fidel Castro took control of Cuba, Villalobos sought asylum in the Embassy of Brazil and on May 9, 1959, he went into exile in Miami.

Alex's father, Jose "Pepe" Villalobos, is an important figure in Cuban American politics as well. According to a Florida Bar article:

> In 1973, The University of Florida College of Law became a pioneer in legal education by creating a program that gave Cuban lawyers in exile the opportunity to become practicing attorneys in the United States.
>
> Villalobos almost did not get into that first class in 1973. The Supreme Court had approved a course of study that would train foreign lawyers who had been admitted to the bar in their home countries. Because of his defiance on the day of his swearing-in ceremony, Villalobos was never admitted to the Cuban bar. Under the rules, he did not qualify for the Cuban American Lawyers Program. After some impromptu lobbying, Villalobos got the chance to make his case before the Supreme Court, which ruled in his favor.

Villalobos went onto being appointed by Florida Governor Bob Graham to a judicial nominating committee, which he later chaired. Villalobos was elected president of the Cuban American Bar Association and has received many well-earned and deserving accolades. Today, Pepe serves as of counsel for Akerman, a law firm with 700 lawyers across 24 U.S. cities.

Alex Villalobos went on to win the election, serving eight years in the Florida House of Representatives, and almost made history as the first Cuban American to serve as Florida Senate President. Instead of coalescing around Villalobos, one of the Cuban American members, Alex Díaz de la Portilla, along with several other GOP senators, some who were loyal backers of Villalobos, also turned on him, and kept him from achieving his goal. Today, Alex is back in private practice.

THE BEST JOB WAS AROUND THE CORNER

After the 1992 general election, I was out of job and back home in Miami. I had spent the entire campaign season working and not looking for a job. A few months passed, I did odd jobs and tried my hardest to get back into politics and a political job.

In February, a job offer came which I rejected, the opportunity to join the office of a newly elected County Commissioner. I felt that his brand would tarnish mine, and I was in this for the long game. Here I am without a job, I get a job offer, and rejected it. What arrogance, huh? In the end, thank God, it all worked out! I mention this for two reasons: sometimes you need to think long-term, not just short term. You don't want to go from bad to worse. Rejecting the offer kept me available and as a result, it led me to an incredible opportunity.

THE MIAMI-DADE DELEGATION:
THE BEST JOB EVER!

In March of 1993, I interviewed for a secretarial position with the Miami-Dade County Legislative Delegation. I guess it was a step up from my receptionist duties at the Amendment 10 campaign. I was offered the job but was reluctant to take it. This was the mid-1990s, no guy wants to be a secretary. It was embarrassing. My friend Marisel Manteiga took me out for drinks and said, "Take the job! It is your entry into Miami-Dade County. Once inside, you can move around to other jobs. Do not be a fool."

In all honesty, she was a lot more colorful with what she said. I took

Marisel's advice and accepted the job. Six months later, my boss, Virginia Sanchez got promoted and the executive director job became open. State Rep. Rudy Garcia (R-Hialeah) was Chair of the Delegation. I lobbied hard for the job!

Everyone who had the job before went on to great success in Miami. You worked with 20 state representatives, seven state senators, the county manager, county mayor, and 13 county commissioners. It is still my favorite job, and I have been very fortunate to have had some great jobs in my lifetime!

Sometime in the fall of 1993, after some political maneuvering, and lots of nudging from Miguel De Grandy, Rep. Garcia appointed me as the Delegations executive director. I felt like I won the Florida lottery!

I served as Executive Director of the Dade Delegation until 1996, long enough to complete my B.A. in Liberal Studies from Barry University. It took me nine years to finish community college. It took me 18 months to finish my B.A. Interesting to see what can be accomplished when one is focused and wants it really badly!

During my time at the Dade Delegation, I was appointed once and re-appointed three consecutive times. I worked for two Republican house members, Rudy Garcia and Alex Villalobos, as well as for two Democrats, State Senators Bill Turner and Ron Silver.

By the way, I never thought I would work with Alex Villalobos again. That is the thing about politics, you never know when you will work for someone again, but if you did a great job the first time around, chances are they will recruit or, in my case, keep you, when the opportunity presents itself again.

At the Delegation, I really learned how diverse Miami-Dade County was. From Homestead and Florida City to Aventura and Golden Beach, it is amazing where an hour's drive takes you. I learned a lot during those three and half years at the Dade Delegation, including how to produce annual reports, hold public hearings, deal with the local media (TV, radio, and print), and produce a weekly public affairs program seen all over the state of Florida. The most important thing I learned was how to have a good relationship with over 40 elected and appointed officials, all of whom thought they were my boss. More importantly, I learned how to be bipartisan.

"Baseball Card," Circa 1994 or 1995.

I also learned the true meaning and understanding of diversity, equity and inclusion (DE&I). Miami has always been the most diverse city south of New York, within the greater African American community, you have Bahamians, Jamaican, and Haitians. The geographic diversity that exists between Homestead and Aventura, or Miami Beach and Hialeah could not have been more stark. On a religious front, the Delegation was very diverse, with Catholic, Jewish, and Baptist members.

I so enjoyed working with all the members of the Delegation, including John Cosgrove, Larcenia Bullard, Daryl Jones, and Ron Saunders—all from South Miami Dade County and the Florida Keys. I was also able to work with some of Miami's most popular African American lawmakers like Carri and Kendrick Meek, Jimmy Bush, Jimmy Burke and Berly Roberts-Burke, Senator Bill Turner, Jefferson and Darryl Reeves, Willie

Logan, among others. It is not unusual to see public roads and buildings named in their honor.

And when it came to the Jewish members of the Delegation, mostly representing Miami Beach, North Dade, and Aventura, I worked with some political icons like Elaine Gordon, Jack Gordon, Mike Abrams, and Elaine Bloom, who, at my going away party from the Delegation, gave me best compliment I could have received. She thought I was registered an independent (no party affiliation) and not a Republican.

It was really important for me to ensure that all 27 elected Dade Delegation members I worked for felt I was fair and nonpartisan. That regardless of their political party affiliation, or my political affiliation, I would always do my best to serve them, honor them, always with the County's best interest at heart.

THE POLITICS OF PERSONAL DESTRUCTION

I grew up during a time in Florida and Miami politics where "consensus" and "working across party lines" was a good thing. Bipartisanship was a good thing. No shame in that game. Democrats and Republicans "fought" during the day, yet gathered at night to drink and dine with each other. Politics was not personal. It was philosophical. I wish we could go back to that time. I feel much more was accomplished back then than today. When I first started working in politics, I was really naïve. I was shocked to learn that it doesn't always smell like roses and feel like a beautiful day at the beach. Politics can be a rough and brutal sport to play.

In modern political history, it is President Bill Clinton during the Monica Lewinsky scandal who used the phrase "the politics of personal destruction." For some reason, that phrase has always stuck with me.

While serving as Executive Director (ED) of the Dade Delegation, I also had the opportunity to work closely with the 13 county commissioners. One of the commissioners I got to know well was Arthur E. Teele, Jr.

Teele, a Florida native, served as the executive responsible for the Urban Mass Transportation (UMT) Administration (now known as the Federal Transit Administration), from 1981 to 1983, under President

Ronald Reagan. While at UMT, Teele directed over $200 million dollars to Miami to help cover the costs of building the Metrorail and Metromover.

In March 1993, he was elected to the Miami-Dade County Commission and served as the Commission's chair. It was during this time that I got to know and work with him. Teele was an African American Republican. Upon his election I reached out to him, offering my assistance and willing to share my knowledge of Miami and Florida politics. He was gracious and throughout the next couple of years, we developed a nice friendship. In 1996, Teele resigned from the county commission to run for mayor of Miami-Dade County, against incumbent, Alex Penelas, a Democrat. Teele quickly pivoted after his loss, and in November 1997, he was elected to a four-year term as a commissioner for the City of Miami. In December of 1997, I relocated to Atlanta, Georgia and over the next few months and years, our friendship slowly dissipated.

On July 27, 2005, Art walked a few blocks from his water view condominium behind the old Omni Hotel to The Miami Herald's offices, and standing in the lobby, shot himself. According to a *Miami Herald* article:

> Wearing a dark suit, a light-blue shirt and a crimson tie, Teele [...] entered The Herald lobby at about 6 p.m., and within minutes pulled a gun from a green canvas bag.
>
> Felix Nazco, 35, the security guard, said before pulling the gun Teele told him: "Tell DeFede to tell my wife I love her," referring to Miami Herald columnist Jim DeFede.
>
> Teele then stood with the gun to his head and gazed out at the street through the lobby's glass doors. As police arrived, he shot himself, security guard Eduardo Pavon said. Teele fell on his back. The pistol clattered across the terrazzo floor. (Yanez, 2005)

The next day, the *Miami Herald* published the photo of Teele, lying on the floor, with blood all around his head. While I respect free speech and the rights of journalist to publish stories, I thought then, and still think, it was a disgraceful act by the newspaper. From my POV, what little dignity Teele had left, the *Miami Herald* took it by posting the photo. Shame on them!

In doing research for this book, I watched *Miami Noir*, a documentary about Teele's final days that concentrated on his suicide. Produced by two University of Miami film students, the documentary "re-examined the scandal in the context of political pressures from the Florida State Attorney's Office during Jeb Bush's administration that raised concerns about the motives for the persecution of Art Teele." I would encourage you to watch the short (under an hour) documentary and decide for yourself.

Although Teele was convicted of corruption by threat against a public servant, posthumously, his case was appealed and his conviction was overturned, exonerating him of all charges. There could be some truth to the allegations brought against Teele. I am not blinded by our friendship, but the bottom line is that we will never know because Art made sure of that in a most powerful and dramatic way.

Art's suicide was the first time I experienced up close and personal the real toll politics can take on a person. It seemed like Art's political enemies were trying to destroy him. I can only imagine the distraught and despair he must have felt. It had to be intense.

It's been 23 years since his suicide (July 2005). What he sought in life, a reputation restored, he received after his death. RIP Authur Teele.

Chapter 7
HISTORY MAKERS, ICONS, AND LAWBREAKERS

I am sort of glad that when I was younger and when it came to important matters, I have not been "the first." Someone has always been there before and paved the way. Not that I could not manage it. I have been through a lot of challenges in my life. Believe me, I have been tested, and quite often. But it is always nice to have a roadmap.

THE FIRSTS

In this chapter, I highlight Cuban Americans who were the first in elective or appointed office: the pioneers and trailblazers. I also highlight all the Cuban Americans in the Florida Legislature between 1980 to 1988. I included non-Cubans who were also "first" and helpful to the Cuban legislators. Lastly, I will share with you the lobbyists who were important players in ensuring Cuban Americans were successful in Tallahassee. In the legislative process, lobbyists play a very important role in the political and legislative process.

I am a broken record when it comes to saying how proud I am to have "grown up" around the first group of Cuban Americans who were elected to various offices, in particular the Florida Legislature.

Collectively, they paved the way for the rest to follow, and continue to open the doors of opportunities for others. And so many Cuban Americans have gone through those doors and continue making history!

ELVIN MARTINEZ

According to my research, attorney Elvin Martinez, a Democrat, was the first Hispanic elected to the Florida Legislature. He was elected State Representative in 1966, representing the Tampa area. My guess is that Martinez did not identify as Cuban, but as Spanish. At that time, and maybe still today, a lot of Hispanics from Tampa identify as Spanish, even though their families came from or through Cuba prior to settling down in Florida. I am not sure why that is.

Rep. Martinez served in the Florida House from 1966 to 1998. In 1998, Florida Governor Lawton Chiles appointed Martinez to a vacant seat on the Hillsborough County Court. Rep. Martinez is quoted saying, "It's something I've had in my mind a long time … I think every lawyer dreams of being a judge."

MAURICE FERRÉ

A year later, Martinez was joined by fellow Democrat Maurice Ferré from Miami. The second Hispanic elected to the Florida House of Representatives—and the first Hispanic from Miami to serve in the legislature, and probably the first Puerto Rican born individual to serve in the Florida Legislature.

Ferré would go on to blaze political trails as the first Hispanic to serve on the City of Miami City Council (1967-1968), and as both the first Puerto Rican born Mayor of a U.S. city and the first Hispanic Mayor in the City of Miami (1973-1985). He also served on the Miami-Dade County Commission from 1993-1996. It was during this time that I worked with him closely—what an honor.

Ferré was known—and is still known, in my opinion—as a visionary and many credit him for revitalizing Miami's downtown with new, shiny buildings which redefined Miami's skyline in the 1970s and 1980s. Ferré took Miami from a sleepy little town on the water to an international city and the gateway to Latin America.

I have always wondered and have been surprised that Ferré was not appointed to a Cabinet position or an ambassadorship by Clinton. As the highest-ranking Puerto Rican and Miamian, it would have been a no-brainer. He is probably the most visionary political leader that I have worked with.

I recently had the opportunity to connect with his daughter, Meme Ferré, an artist in the abstract expressionist style, and the driver behind Florida International University's Maurice A. Ferré Institute for Civic Leadership. Meme shared with me something I was not aware of and had never heard before. The Ferré family "are French that went to Cuba, then escaped during the Spanish American War to Puerto Rico and came to Miami in the 1940s. Maurice Ferré was always super proud of his Cuban roots." She went on to tell me that, "The family gave homes to the Catholic Archdioceses during Operation Peter Pan, and our Cuban Grandfather gave an enormous amount of land in Puerto Rico that became the Pontifical Catholic University in Ponce. He was a Caballero de Malta of the Cuban Order." Thank you, Meme, for sharing.

MANOLO REBOSO

According to a *New York Times* article dated November 17, 1973:

> For the first time since the Cuban exodus to the United States began in the early 1960s, former Cuban refugees who are now American citizens have made their political influence felt here in local elections.

> The Cuban vote has been termed the principal factor in the election last week of Maurice A. Ferre as Mayor of Miami and this Tuesday of Manolo Reboso as a City Commissioner. Both are Democrat.
>
> Mr. Reboso, a 38-year-old Havana-born engineer, is believed to be the first former Cuban refugee elected to public office in this country

I never had the chance to meet Mr. Reboso. While during research for this book, I did have the opportunity to speak with his son's office who confirmed that his dad was the first Cuban to serve on the City of Miami Commission. Mr. Reboso was definitely a pioneer when it comes to Cuban American politics. I am sorry I never had the opportunity to meet him.

JORGE VALDES

Valdes is believed to be the first Cuban-born elected mayor of a U.S. city (1978) and the first Cuban born on the Miami-Dade County Commission (1981), by appointment. He served on the Sweetwater City Council in 1977, making him one of the first Cuban born Americans elected to public office. There is a distinction between Cuban-born and Cuban American.

According to a *Miami Herald* story, "In 1961, Jorge boarded a makeshift raft from his home in Matanzas, Cuba, and set sail for South Florida. Once settled, he would join the U.S. Army and raise four children with his wife in Miami" (Cohen, 2014).

Seventeen years after that trip, Valdes, then a 38-year-old building contractor and public relations agent known for his dapper dress and white hair, made history when he became the first Cuban-born mayor of an American city, Sweetwater. Unfortunately, Valdes' story does not have a fairytale ending.

Valdes served on the commission until he was unseated in 1990 by a young upstart named Alex Penelas, then a Hialeah city councilman who would go on to become the first Cuban American mayor of Miami-Dade County six years later. That year, Valdes was under federal investigation involving allegations that he had accepted $40,000 from developers to vote to rezone and then help sell a parcel of land in West Miami-Dade. Valdes lost his re-election campaign, denied the allegations, and was not indicted. He briefly moved to Venezuela before returning to Miami.

Valdes passed away on October 20, 2014, at the age of 74.

JOE CAROLLO

According to a *New York Times* story:

> In 1979, at the age of 24, Mr. Carollo became Miami's youngest city commissioner. Four years later, in a gambit local politicians still talk of, Mr. Carollo refused to endorse Maurice Ferre for city mayor, a race that Mr. Ferre won, and was called a double-crosser by Ferre supporters. He also angered many Blacks by voting to dismiss Miami's first Black city manager.
>
> In 1987, he failed to win re-election as a commissioner, then lost a race for the Dade County Commission.

Carollo would serve Mayor of the City of Miami twice: from 1996 to 1997 and again from 1998 to 2001. He was City Manager for the City of Doral for a brief stint. In 2017, he ran successfully for election to the Miami city commission, where he serves today.

During his 40 years of off-and-on public service, he's been labeled, or some would say, has earned the moniker "Crazy Joe" for his loud, public outbursts, a live, televised "double-cross" non-endorsement, a domestic violence incident, and other numerous actions, including a recent (2023) federal trial where a jury decided he would pay a large sum for abusing his authority.

Carollo is expected to appeal the verdict. The one unanswered question is who is liable for payment: Carollo or the City of Miami, who has already spent millions on defending Carollo. His current term as Miami City Commissioner ends in November of 2025. Will Carollo run or retire? His voters loved him, so Carollo's guilty verdict could energize his political base.

XAVIER SUAREZ

With his November 13, 1985, election as Mayor, City of Miami, Xavier became the first Cuban-born to serve in that role. This was a huge deal for Cubans in Miami, to have one of their own, born on the Island, now Mayor of Miami, the epicenter of all things (free) Cuba. Suarez, who defeated Maurice Ferre in the 1985 election, would go on to win re-election in 1987 and in 1989, where he served his final term (4 years) as Mayor of Miami.

A practicing attorney, in 2011, Suarez was elected Miami-Dade County Commissioner, serving until term limits forced him out in November 2020. Suarez ran for Miami-Dade County mayor, coming in fourth (4th) place.

While back in Miami and at Carnival Corporation, from 2014 – 2019, I really enjoyed working with Mayor Suarez again. Always willing to listen and be upfront with you. You cannot ask for more from a public servant.

His son, Francis Suarez, a registered Republican, is Miami's current Mayor. Francis was born in Miami—a native! The apple did not fall far from that political tree.

On Thursday, June 15, 2023, Mayor Suarez announced his candidacy for President of the United States. He is the first Hispanic on the Republican side to file paperwork. On Tuesday, August 29, 2023, after not qualifying for the first GOP Presidential Debate, Suarez suspended his campaign for President, leaving the field without a Latino candidate.

ALEX PENELAS

First elected to the City of Hialeah as a Council member, at the age of 25, Alex went on to become the second Cuban American on the Miami-Dade County Commission, beating the first Cuban American, Jorge Valdes.

Alex then became the first Cuban American Mayor of Miami-Dade County, serving from October 1996 to November 2004. He is a registered Democrat.

ROBERTO CASAS

Roberto Casas is the first Cuban American elected to the Florida Legislature. A Republican from Hialeah, Casas was elected to the Florida House of Representatives during a special election in January 1982. Casas was elected to the Florida Senate in 1988 and served until 2000. He is also the first Cuban American to serve as Florida Senate President Pro Tempore.

Senator Casas passed away on December 16, 2021, at the age of 90. To honor the memory of former Senator Casas, Governor Ron DeSantis directed flags to be flown at half-staff at the Miami-Dade County Courthouse, Hialeah City Hall, and at the State Capitol in Tallahassee, Florida. A well-deserved honor. RIP Senator.

HUMBERTO CORTINA

The first Bay of Pigs veteran to serve in the Florida Legislature, Cortina was elected in 1982, representing Miami's Little Havana. He beat a young, smart Democrat named Lincoln Díaz-Balart. More on him later in the book. Cortina only served one term.

Cortina participated in the Bay of Pigs Invasion and was wounded in both legs, captured, and sent to political prison for two years. Upon his return to the U.S., he was commissioned by President Kennedy as an Officer in the U.S. Army.

He obtained a B.A. degree from the University of Florida, where he later served on its Board of Regents. Cortina went on to become a successful entrepreneur, businessman, and most recently political commentator and radio talk show host on TelevisaUnivision radio station.

In 2023, I had the opportunity to have lunch with Rep. Cortina and it was wonderful. He is still as charming as ever, and even funnier that I remember him. During the course of our two- and half-hour lunch with Guarione Díaz, a mutual friend, several "friends" stopped by the table to say hello to Rep. Cortina. To this day, he is still admired by his constituents.

ILEANA ROS-LEHTINEN

History maker extraordinaire. Ileana is the first Hispanic woman to serve in the Florida House of Representatives (1982-1986), the Florida Senate (1986-1989) and in the United States House of Representatives (1989-2019).

She is also the first Republican woman to serve as Chair of the House Foreign Affairs Committee. When first appointed to the Committee, there was no room for her on the dais, so she sat in a chair. We've come a long way baby!

LUIS CARLOS MORSE

A Bay of Pigs veteran, Morse was the first Cuban American to serve as Speaker Pro Temp during the 1996 to 1998 legislative session. He served in the Florida House from 1984 to 1988. Between 1999 and 2002, he served as Deputy Secretary and later Secretary, Florida Department of Elder Affairs.

He defeated incumbent Rep. Humberto Cortina and was defeated by newcomer, Cuban American, Republican Manuel Prieguez.

Morse passed away at the age of 83, on May 28, 2023.

ALBERTO GUTMAN

Al Gutman, if you are in Miami Beach, or Alberto Gutman (pronounced Goot-man), if you are in Little Havana, is the first Cuban American Jewish member elected to the Florida Legislature. An extremely personal, charming young politician, who was able to literally "bridge" the divide between Little Havana's Cuban community and Miami Beach's Jewish community. He did that for years, first as a Member of the Florida House of Representatives (1984-1992) and then as a Florida State Senator (1992-1999).

In 1998, Senator Gutman was indicted on 32 counts for benefiting from a fake healthcare company that he had set up to defraud Medicare of $15,000,000. Gutman then resigned his post as Chairman of the Florida Senate Health Care Committee over alleged improprieties in brokering a Medicaid health plan during his term as vice chairman of the committee.

Gutman was charged with conspiracy, money laundering, and witness tampering. He served five years in prison with three years' probation and ordered to pay victims $98,175 in restitution and fined $50,000. His wife, Marci Gutman, got six months of house arrest after pleading guilty for her role in the scheme.

On February 16, 2019, Senator Gutman died at his home surrounded by friends and family. He was 60 years old. Rest in Peace, Al.

RAUL L. MARTINEZ

Elected to the Hialeah City Council in 1977, at the age of 27, and as a Democrat, making him one of the first Cuban Americans elected to political office in the United States.

Raul became the second Cuban American mayor of a U.S. city, Hialeah, Florida, where he would go on to serve for 24 years as mayor— El Alcalde—from 1981 to 2005, never losing an election. Impressive track record!

In April of 1990, Martinez was suspended as mayor of Hialeah, after being indicted on eight federal charges. In March of 1991, Martinez was convicted on six of those eight charges and a judge sentenced him to 10 years. Martinez appealed the decision; an appellate judge ordered a new trial in 1994, and that second trial ended in a hung jury. The third trial resulted in an acquittal and a deadlock on the five remaining counts. During this time, a new U.S. Attorney was appointed by President Clinton, a Democrat named Kendall Coffey, who dropped the remaining five charges. In 2008, Martinez ran unsuccessfully for Florida's 21st congressional district, losing to Lincoln Díaz-Balart.

ROSARIO KENNEDY

Rosario was the first Cuban-born American woman elected to the City of Miami Commission in 1985, defeating incumbent commissioner Demetrio Perez. During her tenure, she was selected as Vice Mayor of the City of Miami.

Kennedy ran unsuccessfully for congress in 1989, losing the Democratic primary to attorney Gerald Richman, who lost the general election to Ileana Ros-Lehtinen, after a nasty campaign where Mr. Richman was quoted as saying, "Let's keep this an American seat."

I would argue we did by electing the first female Cuban *American* to the U.S. Congress!

ANNIE BETANCOURT

Annie is the first Cuban-born woman Democrat to win election to the Florida House of Representatives, serving from 1994 through 2002. She is the third Cuban American woman elected to the Florida House, following in the footsteps of Republican Arnhilda Gonzalez-Quevedo (Badia today) and of course, Ileana Ros-Lehtinen.

PAUL L. CEJAS

Ambassador Cejas is the first Cuban American to serve on the Miami-Dade County School Board, winning election in 1984. He is also the first Cuban American to serve as Chair, Miami-Dade School Board.

In 1998, President Clinton appointed Cejas United States Ambassador to Belgium, where he served until January 3, 2001. Prior to public service, Cejas was founder and CEO of CareFlorida Health Systems. Today, Cejas is a well-known art collector and chairman and CEO of PLC Investments, Inc.

ROSA CASTRO-FEINBERG

Rosa Castro-Feinberg, Ph.D., is the first Latina elected County-wide, and for eight years, the only Hispanic to serve on the Miami-Dade School Board.

First appointed by Florida Governor Bob Graham (D) in 1986, she won re-election in 1988 and 1992. During her 10-year tenure, Dr. Castro-Feinberg also served as Chair of the School Board.

Considered an educational expert, after the school board, she went to teach and retire from Florida International University (FIU).

THE DÍAZ DE LA PORTILLA FAMILY

I would bet $100 bucks that the Díaz de la Portilla family is the first and only Cuban American political family to have served in four different levels of government:

1. Miami-Dade County Commission (Miguel)
2. Miami-Dade County School Board (Renier)
3. City of Miami Commission (Alex)
4. Florida Legislature:
   - Florida House: Alex and Renier
   - Florida Senate: Alex and Miguel

Quite the political feat!

As I stated earlier, in running for public office in Miami, it helps if your family was in politics in Cuba, prior to Castro, and that's the case with the Díaz de la Portilla's, who are all Republicans.

Alex, Miguel, and Reiner's great-grandfather served in the Cuban Senate, while two of their great-uncles served simultaneously in the Cuban House of Representatives.

ALEX DÍAZ DE LA PORTILLA

Elected to the Florida House of Representatives (District 115) in 1994, serving through 2000. Alex was succeeded by his brother, Renier Díaz de la Portilla.

In 2000, Alex was elected to the Florida Senate (Districts 34 and 36) where he served until 2010. Alex was succeeded by his other brother, Miguel Díaz de la Portilla.

Alex served on the City of Miami Commission, a position he was elected to at the end of 2021. Alex is the only elected official I know who has been succeeded twice, by two different brothers, to two state offices.

On Thursday, September 14, 2023, Alex was arrested by the Florida Department of Law Enforcement (FDLE), charged with 10 plus criminal counts. On Friday evening, September 15, Florida Governor DeSantis signed an executive order which removed Díaz de la Portilla from office. In spite of his removal, Díaz de la Portilla ran for re-election and after a run-off, he lost by 281 vote.

MIGUEL DÍAZ DE LA PORTILLA

Miguel first ran for political office in 1992, winning election to the Miami-Dade County Commission, where he served from 1993 to 2000. From November 2010 to November 2016, Miguel served as a member of the Florida Senate (Districts 36 and 40). Holding the same senate district as his brother Alex.

The first time I met Miguel was in 1992. I was working on the campaign of Just Luis Pozo, who was also running for the County Commission. As Miguel reminded me, there were more than a handful of candidates running in the district. Unfortunately for me and Justo, we came third in the run-off. Miguel went on to win the election, beating Joe Garcia. That election was the start of Miguel's public service to our community.

RENIER DÍAZ DE LA PORTILLA

Renier served on the Miami-Dade County School board twice, from 1996 to 1998 and from 2006 to 2012. He also served in the Florida House of Representatives, succeeding his brother Alex. Renier served one term from 2000 to 2002 (District 115). Renier recently ran (2022) an unsuccessful campaign for Miami-Dade County judgeship.

The Diaz de la Portilla's service to our community, carrying on their family's legacy of public service, and their ability to serve at the different levels of government is duly noted!

KATHERINE "KATHY" FERNANDEZ-RUNDLE

Kathy is the first Cuban American State Attorney in the state of Florida. She was appointed by Florida Governor Chiles in 1993 upon Janet Reno's resignation. Reno served as President Clinton's Attorney General from 1993 to 2001.

Kathy is a second-generation attorney. Her father, Dr. Carlos Benito Fernandez, served as Miami's first Hispanic judge and a founder of the Cuban American Bar Association (CABA). In 1993, she was elected CABA's first female president. Prior to her appointment as State Attorney, she was an Assistant State Attorney, serving as Chief Assistant State Attorney and Legal Counsel to the Dade County Grand Jury.

GOVERNOR BOB MARTINEZ

Robert Martinez served as the 40th governor of Florida from 1987 to 1991. Martinez is not Cuban. I believe he considers himself of "Spanish Decent," and so I chose to include him in the book. During his tenure, he was very helpful to the Cuban community and Cuban American legislators.

Martinez was born and raised in Tampa, Florida, attended the University of Tampa, and began his career as an educator in the local public school system and then the University of Tampa. In 1965, he was named the director of the local teachers' union, a position he held during the Florida statewide teachers' strike of 1968.

He first entered politics with an unsuccessful run for mayor of Tampa in 1974, then won the office in Tampa's next mayoral election in 1979 and was reelected in 1983. During his second term as mayor, Martinez switched his party affiliation from Democrat to Republican, upsetting some supporters in heavily Democratic Tampa.

He resigned the position in 1986 to focus on his ultimately successful campaign for the governor of Florida. His single term as governor was controversial due to the passage and repeal of an unpopular state sales tax on services and an anti-obscenity campaign targeting Miami rappers 2 Live Crew, who later recorded a derogatory song attacking Martinez. He lost his reelection campaign to U.S. Senator Lawton Chiles in 1990.

After his time as governor, Martinez was appointed Director of the Office of National Drug Control Policy by President George H.W. Bush. Martinez held that position from 1991 until 1993 when he returned to Tampa and became a business consultant and a board member of several local educational organizations.

Martinez was the first time this Cuban exile got so close to a power player like the governor. How many governors know the name of a legislative aide? How many twenty-somethings have that kind of relationship with a governor? For me, our relationship demonstrated that regardless of where you came from, you can establish relationships with very powerful people. And most importantly, use the relationship for good.

Governor Bob Martinez and me. Photos taken 10 years apart: 1990 and 2000.

ALFREDO DURAN

According to a *New York Times* news article, at the time he was elected, Duran, 39, was the first Democratic party chairman from Miami-Dade County and first and highest elected official of Cuban descent (in the Democratic Party).

The Cuban born Miami lawyer, who fought in the Bay of Pigs invasion, was a relative newcomer to party politics. Democratic leaders believed that Duran would attract thousands of new Cuban American votes to the Democratic Party given his role as the national Latin coordinator of Carter's Presidential campaign.

ALBERTO "AL" CARDENAS

This Cuban American lawyer and lifelong Republican became the first to serve as Chair of the Florida Republican party, and the only Hispanic to date.

Al worked for President Reagan (transition team) and served as a Presidential appointee under Reagan and George H.W. Bush's Administrations. Today, Cardenas continues to practice law and is a highly respected and regular political commentator on several of the Sunday morning public affairs shows.

MARCO ANTONIO RUBIO

Part of the second wave of Cuban Americans elected to office, Rubio makes history by becoming the first Cuban American elected Speaker of the Florida House of Representatives, serving from November 21, 2006, to November 18, 2008.

His first foray into public service is in the city where he grew up in, West Miami. A middle-class, small enclave located between the City Beautiful, Coral Gables to the east, unincorporated Miami-Dade County to the west, and the City of Miami to the north. I know the area well, growing up a few blocks to the west, but having many friends and family in West Miami. Marco's first foray into politics is as a member of the West Miami City Commissioner. From there he is elected to the Florida House of Representatives, serving from 2000 to 2008.

On January 3, 2011, Marco began his first term as a United States Senator from Florida. In 2016, Marco ran for President of the United States. Unfortunately, he dropped out of the race after losing the Florida Presidential primary to Donald Trump, who, as we know, would go on to win the Presidency.

Today, at 51, he is the Senior Senator from Florida. No doubt you will call him Governor Rubio one day. I believe Marco can be the first Hispanic Vice President or President. Time is on his side.

CUBAN AMERICANS IN THE FLORIDA LEGISLATURE

The following section highlights the first Cuban-born and Cuban Americans elected to the Florida Legislature by election cycle through the 1998 election (serving through 2000).

Between February 1989 and December 1999, I had the incredible opportunity to work with so many Cuban American elected officials who were making history as it was happening. I cannot tell you how humbled and honored I am to have been there and to have had a "front row" seat to witness all that was happening.

The first elected or appointed Cuban Americans arrived in Tallahassee in 1982 to take their respective seats in the Florda Legislature: Roberto Casas, a realtor from Hialeah, Humberto Cortina, a business executive from Little Havana, and Ileana Ros, a schoolteacher from West Dade County. All three Republicans. Casas won a special election on January 27, 1982, making him the first Cuban American Republican elected to the Florida House of Representatives. Cortina and Ros were elected during a regular election on Tuesday, November 2, 1982.

Please see Appendix A for the list of Cuban Americans elected to the Florida Legislature from 1980 to 1998.

Between 1982 and 1989, in just seven years, over two dozen Cuban Americas—all Republicans—would serve in the Florida Legislature and Miami would elect its first Cuban American in Congress, Ileana Ros-Lehtinen, making history as the first Latina in Congress.

Of the nearly two dozen Florida legislators, only two were women, both Republicans. In 1994, Annie Betancourt becomes the first Cuban American Democrat woman to serve in the Florida House.

State Senators Alex Villalobos (R-West Dade), Rudy Garcia (R-Hialeah) and Alex Díaz de la Portilla (R-Miami), circa 2004.

Please see Appendix B for the Cuban Americans elected (and re-elected) to the Florida Legislature from 1992-2000. As the first 10-12 years neared, a new, young group of Cuban Americans and non-Cubans are elected, and with that, comes more turnover.

"Old School" Clerk's Manual. These were very handy as they Included all the members of the Legislature: photo & bios.

THE "JOHN ELLIS BUSH" YEARS IN FLORIDA POLITICS

Florida's Cuban American community, and in particular, its Republican elected and appointed officials benefited greatly, in my opinion, by the "JEB years." The Bush family (President George H.W. Bush, President George Bush, and Governor Jeb Bush) have played an important role in Florida's politics over the last 25 years. As a state, Florida has a direct line into the Vice President's Office, and then into the President's office. That's powerful!

If you don't understand Miami-Dade County's voters and politics, and just look at the voter registrations, you could make the assumption that there is probably no way a Republican could win an election in Miami, where the largest number of registered voters are Democrat (512,853), followed by No Party Affiliation (464,066), and then Republican voters (439,256), as of March 1, 2024. You would be wrong!

Miami-Dade County's voter registration has leaned Democrat for years, and No Party Affiliation (NPA) continues to outnumber "registered" Republican party (as of March 1, 2024). The first and last Florida Republican governor to win Miami-Dade County was Gov. Jeb Bush in 2000.

Although I have no real proof or research, just common sense and my personal experience in politics, the rise of GOP Cuban Americans in Florida politics aligned nicely with the rise of Jeb Bush's successful career in politics and elected office in Florida.

Jeb Bush and his family (wife Columba and three young children) relocated to Miami, Florida, in 1981, the year after his father was elected Vice President of the United States. Jeb goes into business with a Cuban American business icon named Armando Codina, a successful real-estate developer. At that point, there were only a few Cuban Americans elected to political office. There were zero in the Florida Legislature nor Congress.

Young Jeb becomes active in South Florida Republican politics, being elected as Chair of the Republican Party in Dade County (1984-86) and as Florida's commerce secretary (1987-88). In 1988, Jeb worked on his father's successful presidential campaign. Obviously not Cuban American, our community adopted Jeb as our own. Not bad to have the President's son in your backyard.

I've had the opportunity to meet Jeb over the years and he was always nice, down-to-earth, a great sense of humor, and caring person. We had mutual friends in common like Adriana Comellas-Macretti and Tony Cotarelo, along with a few others. This was before he ran for Florida Governor in 1994, the same year his brother, George W. Bush ran for governor of Texas.

Jeb was defeated by "Walking" Lawton Chiles, a former Florida U.S. Senator. During their last televised debate, Senator Chiles turned to Jeb Bush and said, "But let me tell you something about the old liberal. The old he-coon walks just before the light of day."

Millions of Floridians did not understand the reference, but the quote gained significant media attention. In Miami, we thought Senator Chiles had lost his mind. I don't know a Republican Cuban American who knew what Chiles meant. Little did we know it was a political "dog whistle" to the older, white established voters in central and northern Florida. And it worked!

In politics, a dog whistle is "political shorthand for a phrase that may sound innocuous to some people, but which also communicates something more insidious either to a subset of the audience or outside of the audience's conscious awareness—a covert appeal to some noxious set of views" (Olasov, 2016).

It was a close election. Chiles won by 1.5%. He is the last elected Democrat to serve as Governor of Florida. Upon Governor Chiles' death, as mandated in Florida's constitution, his Lt. Governor, Buddy McKay succeeded him. Since 1998, every Governor elected in Florida has been a Republican.

Jeb ran for Governor in 1998 and won re-election, serving eight years. I would say it was the first time in modern political history that a "Son of Miami," someone who understood Cubans, Miamians, and Florida Republicans, would serve as governor. It was cool to see Jeb as Governor, and even cooler that he remembered your name! In politics, it is those little things—remembering names of people you are not friends with, but you know they are involved in politics or that they matter in the political process.

In 2016, Jeb ran for President of the United States. In February of 2016, just before the Florida Republican primary, he suspended his campaign for President. It was a sad and disappointing day for many of us, and the end of the "I am a Bush Republican" era.

Today, Jeb and his wife reside in Miami, along with their son, Jeb Jr., and daughter, Noelle. His son, George P., has resided in Texas for many years and served as commissioner, Texas General Land Office, from 2015 to 2023.

(Photo Credit: Florida Memory)

I'M A LOBBYISTS. I AM HERE TO HELP.

No book on politics could be complete without including lobbyists. Any successful elected official, public servant, or politician—whatever they call themselves—has had to work with a lobbyist in order to achieve their success.

Lobbyists have and will always be part of the political and legislative process. They are needed in the process. They bring expertise and experience to the process that freshly minted elected officials do not have. The really good ones know where the "bodies are buried" and who buried them.

I am proud to have worked as a lobbyist for both Waste Management and Ford Motor Company. It is a badge of honor, a proud moment in my career. To represent a Fortune 500 company in the political process is a huge responsibility. I am also proud of the "lobbying" work I have done on behalf of a lot of nonprofits that I have served or worked with.

Florida's growth has fueled the growth of many sectors, including the lobbying ranks. As Cuban Americans grew in representation and power, through holding various committee chairmanships, they need lobbyists to help them achieve success.

In this section, I will highlight six lobbyist that were there from the beginning:

- Ronald L. Book
- Doug Bruce
- Humberto "Bert" Gomez
- Fausto Gomez
- Robert "Bob" Levy
- Ana Mollinedo Mims

RONALD L. BOOK

Ron Book is a brilliant, smooth talker, 24/7 work horse who, as the saying goes, could sell ice to an ice factory. I first met Ron in 1989 when I worked for Rep. Miguel De Grandy. Over the next 10 years, I got to know him better, personally and professionally, and this man is solid.

Nothing shakes him. What I admire most about him is all the pro bono work he has done over the years, and his love for Miami-Dade County.

Ron Book was also always on our side, helping the newly elected Cuban Americans navigate the political waters and the good old boy system that was Tallahassee in the 1980s and 1990s. It is a place he grew up in in the 1970s and understood exceptionally well.

In 2023, Ron was recognized with the Florida Bar President's Pro Bono Service Award for 2023 for the 11th Judicial Circuit. Well-earned and deserved.

DOUG BRUCE

I do not recall when I first met Doug, but it would have been around 1989. He was a partner at the lobbying shop of Plante, Bruce, and Adams. Ken Plante was a former Majority Leader in the Florida Senate and Carl Adams worked in the legislature. Doug also worked in the legislature. Like all great lobbyists, you need to work in the legislature and understand the legislative process.

After a few years, Doug and I became good friends. I would school him on all things Cuban and Miami politics, and he would school me on the process and people's history in the process. We would also introduce each other to others around the state, expanding our networks.

When you can learn from someone and they from you, it really strengthens the friendship, and work associates become almost family. I miss spending time with Doug and our many conversations and our friendship.

HUMBERTO "BERT" GOMEZ

There are three "Cuban" lobbyists from the late 1980s and early 1990s that were part of the historic rise of Cuban Americans in Florida politics, and Bert is one of them. Bert's corporate pedigree is impressive: Dow Chemicals, Reynolds American, Univision Communications, and most recently Becker, a powerful and influential Florida law firm.

While at Univision, Bert led and managed Univision's Washington, D.C., office, being one of the few Latinos to hold such a position of power in the beltway.

Today, Bert is based in Becker's newly opened Sacramento, CA, office. His wife Susie is VP of Legislative Affair for AT&T and is enjoying being back home in California.

FAUSTO GOMEZ

The next Cuban—and no relation to Bert—is Fausto Gomez. Fausto started his career as a political aide to Maurice Ferre, the City of Miami's first Hispanic mayor. He cut his political teeth as Florida International University (FIU)'s in-house lobbyist in the 1980s. In 1987, he founded Barker Gomez Associates, where he has spent the last 30 plus years, building an incredible lobbying shop with dozens of high-prolife clients, local municipalities, and Fortune 500 corporations.

In November of 2022, Gomez decided to throw his hat in the political ring and ran for mayor of Key Biscayne, one of the wealthiest and smallest municipalities in Miami, where he now resides and is a former municipal client of his firm's. Gomez lost the election.

ROBERT "BOB" LEVY

We lost Bob in April 2016, at the age of 67, to cancer. For almost 40 years Bob worked the hallways of Tallahassee on behalf of his clients. He mentored so many in the old school art of lobbying and had a hand in electing more judges to the bench from Miami-Dade County than anyone else I know.

He was one of the founders of "Dade Days" in Tallahassee. The once-a-year extravaganza where on the steps of the Capitol, he served Paella to over 2,000 people for lunch!

When I moved back to Miami in 2014, Bob was one of the first people I reconnected with, along with Monty Trainer and of course Dianne Raulson—Ms. Dade Days!

To the Cubans, Bob was on our side. Inclusion and friendship were what I remember most about him. His mantra was, *"We support candidates on both sides of the aisle and try to not get bogged down in the politics of the process."*

Bob served our country during the Vietnam War. In recognition of his service, he was awarded the Silver Star, the Bronze Star, and three Purple Hearts.

In all my years in politics, I have never met anyone like Bob. His love and respect for the process and those in it is admirable. His bipartisanship is remarkable. To Bob, strangers were friends he had not met yet. First class all the way. Rest in Peace my friend!

ANA MOLLINEDO MIMS

It was rare to see a Latina lobbyist in the 1980s or early 1990s. The only one I can recall is my good friend, Cuban American Ana Mollinedo Mims, who at the time was lobbying for the Florida Retail Federation and later for Monsanto and Eli Lilly.

Ana is a trailblazer extraordinaire! She has been at the VP level or above at Cemex, Starwood, and Cable & Wireless Communications. She has also served as the Executive Director of the Martin Luther King Center, on numerous national and international nonprofit and for-profit boards and as a senior executive on several start-ups.

Lobbyists often get a bad rap, and I can see why. My experience is that they do more good than bad. A great lobbyist understands both sides of the issue, can explain it in simple terms, and also takes into consideration what would best for the elected official, and for their client(s). Most importantly, a great lobbyist knows the art of compromise, that relationships are key to their success, and that you play the long game. No one will be with you 100% of the time, all of the time.

Ana is also an author, writing *Keeping the Faith: How Applying Spiritual Purpose to Your Work Can Lead to Extraordinary Success,* published by Harper Collins/Rayo in 2007.

Chapter 8
ADMIRATION AND RESPECT

ADMIRATION:
A social emotion felt by observing people of competence, talent, or skill exceeding standards. Admiration facilitates social learning in groups. Admiration motivates self-improvement through learning from role-models.

RESPECT:
Respect means that you accept somebody for who they are, even when they're different from you or you don't agree with them. Respect in your relationships builds feelings of trust, safety, and wellbeing. Respect doesn't have to come naturally, it is something you learn.

Regardless of your profession, you are going to work with some really outstanding people who will have a tremendous impact on you and your career. You will also work with some real "winners," as well, but we're going to focus on the positive experiences and people for this chapter. Sometimes the impact is immediate. Sometimes, you may not realize it right away. And sometimes, it may take a few years, during deep times of reflection, to realize how powerful the interactions were and how fortunate you are to have experienced them.

As you may imagine, over the course of a 35 year plus career, there are so many individuals who I could have included. I could write a book just on that alone. Using LinkedIn as my platform, between 2020 and 2021, I highlighted, really celebrated, several of these individuals. I encourage you to read the posts. Because of the posts, I was awarded by LinkedIn with a *"Top Voices"* recognition. Quite the honor!

In this chapter, and in alphabetical order, I write about some of the Cuban American elected and appointed officials who I had the opportunity and pleasure of working with and that I have come to greatly admire and respect. Let me repeat myself: obviously, there are numerous other elected and appointed officials that I admire and respect, but since this book is focused on Cuban Americans, I chose to focus only on this group.

If I have learned nothing else in politics, besides learning how to count, it is that inclusion and diversity is always a winning strategy.

JOAQUIN AVIÑO, P.E.

Sometimes, people come into your life for a short time, but have a powerful impact, and that's the case with Joaquin Aviño. Although he was not the first Cuban American Miami-Dade County Manager, that history was made by his predecessor, Sergio Pereira, Joaquin's appointment almost certainly ensured that for the foreseeable future, Miami-Dade County Managers would be Cuban Americans. And that was the case for the next appointment and future appointments.

As I look back now, I am in awe that at 37 years old, he was handed the reins of county government, which at the time was the largest county government operation in Florida: 2 million residents, 23,000 employees, and a $3.6-billion-dollar budget, or the equivalent of a Fortune 125 company.

Aviño worked as a civil engineer on residential and highway projects before joining the Metro-Dade Building and Zoning Department in 1980. In 1985, he became assistant county manager in charge of nine departments, including public works and planning.

At the age of 44, Aviño announced his resignation as County Manager in October of 1994, effective January 1995. He returned to the private sector with the architectural firm Wolfberg & Alvarez.

The value of an education is priceless. Wish I would have learned this sooner. For a long time, I was not too fond of Joaquin Aviño. I didn't understand why, when he could have waived an educational requirement, he did not. Let me explain.

The year was 1993, and I was working at the Miami-Dade County Legislative Delegation as an assistant for a few months. My salary classification was Executive Secretary III or something like that. The salary was around $25K. My boss at the time, the Delegation's Executive Director (ED) Virginia Sanchez, was promoted to be the County's top lobbyist, and so the ED position would be open. Sometime in the fall of 1993, after some political maneuvering, then Delegation Chairman, State Representative Rudy Garcia, appointed me as ED. I felt like I won the Florida lottery!

A few days into my new role, I went upstairs to the 29th floor to meet with an HR manager to learn about my benefits, new salary, etc. During the meeting, I learned that the role required a college degree, and I did not meet that qualification. I was crushed. HR said I could do the job, but I would be paid at my current level (Executive Legislative Secretary, III, or some similar title).

This being government and politics, I figured there was an exemption: a way to by-pass the system and the fact I didn't have that "stupid little piece of paper" my parents and society had pushed so hard on me to obtain—a college degree. I learned that the way to bypass the requirement was for Joaquin Aviño to sign a waiver. I thought, how easy is that? I will ask the next Delegation Chair to ask the Manager for this little favor, and surely the Manager would do it.

In November of 1993, the Delegation elected State Senator William "Bill" Turner as the next chair. Senator Turner was the first African American to serve on the Miami-Dade School Board and would later make history again by being elected the School Board's first African American Chair. What a privilege it was to work for Sen. Turner.

At the time, I didn't see the irony (or the arrogance) of asking Sen. Turner, an educator, to ask the County Manager to waive the educational requirements. Senator Turner made "the ask" of the County Manager who said, "No. I will not sign the waiver. Carlos needs to go to school and earn his degree."

I was mad. Livid. You name it. I took it personally. I avoided the Manager as best I could.

A few days after Senator Turner had delivered the bad news, I went upstairs to the 29th floor to see the top HR manager, Bonnie Burrell. There had to be another way to bypass the Manager, I thought. I didn't want to give up. She assured me there was no way to bypass Aviño.

Instead of ending our conversation and asking me to leave her office, which she could have given my stupid ask, she shared with me that the County had a partnership with Barry University. All eligible county employees could be reimbursed for up to 50% of their tuition if they received a "C" or better and had approval from their manager. I said to her, "Sign me up!"

While it took me 9 years to attain 60 credits from Miami Dade College, it took me 18 months to complete the last two years of my education—an additional 60 credits—which I did while holding down a full-time job and traveling to Tallahassee for annual committee meetings and the legislative session. Because of Barry's ACE (Adult Continuing Education) program, now called PACE (Professional and Career Education), I was able to "clep" 11 credits from my work experience. I busted my you know what for those 18 months, going to school at night and sometimes taking up to four classes during the summer semesters, but it was all worth it.

On June 17, 1995, I proudly walked across the stage and received my Bachelor of Liberal Studies degree, earning a GPA of 3.25. You can imagine how proud and relieved my mother was. A woman with four degrees—two from Cuba and two from the U.S.—her only son finally, after 11 years, graduated with a college degree!

On Monday, June 19, I went back to the 29th floor to meet with Bonnie, showed her my degree and transcripts, and said to her with the biggest smile on my face, "I finally graduated college. Now double my salary!" Because of Joaquin Aviño's "no" I was "forced" to go back to school and learn a few things, academically and personally. Academically, I found out that I loved philosophy and psychology classes. I realized how lucky I was to have my employer pay for half of my education.

Personally, I never thought I could push myself so hard to accomplish something I had little interest in at the time, an education. Today, I place tremendous value on "el papelito"—Cuban slang for a college degree—and have begun working on a master's degree at Georgetown University.

Obtaining my college degree was one of the best decisions I've ever made. The degree has opened doors for me, such as being hired by Waste Management of Florida, my first corporate job. Without a college degree, I know there's no way Waste Management nor Ford Motor Company would have hired me, and so on, and so on.

Mr. Manager, Sir, thank you so much, and apologies it's taken me all this time to recognize that you had my best interest at heart and that you did the right thing. By saying "No" to a request like mine, you made me a better person, smarter county executive, and leader.

Fast forward to 2018. The photo below is from Barry University's 2018 Distinguished Alumni Awards luncheon. I was one of the honorees! It was wonderful to have my mom, wife, best friends, and my Carnival Corporation family attend. And what a treat to see Sister Jeanne (President of Barry when I attended) and Sister Peggy (her chief of staff) at the luncheon. I love those nuns!

Barry University's 2018 Distinguished Alumni Awards luncheon.

ANNIE BETANCOURT

The "Sparkle" in the middle of the Fireworks!

Most people love fireworks shows. There's something about it that is exciting, new, and fresh, even though you've seen 20 fireworks shows before. As fascinated as we are with the show, maybe we are equally intrigued by a sparkler? Maybe it's because you can hold it in your hand? Maybe it's because you know it's both safe and can be dangerous? Or maybe it's just fun to watch up close?

If I had to describe Annie Betancourt, it would be that sparkler in the middle of the show. She's that enchanting and interesting, you never know where she's coming from, or what she's going to say. She has the energy of 100 sparklers and brings her own drums—timbales in Cuban speak—to the party, along with a cigar. True!

Annie was the first Cuban American Democrat woman to win election to the Florida House of Representatives, serving from 1994 through 2002. She was the third Cuban American woman elected to the Florida House, following in the footsteps of Arnhilda Gonzalez-Quevedo (Badia today) and, of course, Ileana Ros-Lehtinen. In a sea of red, Annie's sparkler burned bright blue!

Prior to her election, Annie had a long and distinguished track record of giving back to the community. This record inspired me to get involved and engaged in the community. There is so much need!

Annie served as Executive Director of the Miami-Dade County Legislative Delegation, the first Cuban to do so. It is the same job I held between 1993 and 1996. In fact, this is how I first met Annie. She stopped by the office to introduce herself, check out the new ED, and share some wisdom and advice.

There's a special kindship that we have. In addition to holding the same role at the County, we are both members of Leadership Florida's Cornerstone program, she Class XI and me Class XV. We have both served on the Cuban American National Council's Board of Directors and have completed an executive education program at the Harvard Business School.

In 2002, Annie decided not to seek re-election to the Florida House and instead she opted to run for Congress, running in the Democratic primary for the newly created 25th congressional seat. The election pitted her against another Cuban American, Republican state representative Mario Diaz-Balart, who was keen to join his brother, Lincoln Díaz-Balart, and Ileana Ros-Lehtinen in Congress.

The Díaz-Balart's, Ros-Lehtinen, and the majority (at that time) of Cuban Americans also supported the U.S. embargo on Cuba. Annie did not, and she wanted to be vocal about it.

According to news articles, Annie sent a letter to the Miami Herald stating, *"The current outdated policy has only served to isolate the Cuban people and has given the Castro regime an excuse for [its] failed economic policies. It is time to frame a changed posture towards Cuba, one that doesn't pander to the Cuban regime but likewise doesn't punish the Cuban people. It is time to put an end to the tired and fruitless formulas that have helped perpetuate the power of a tyrant."* MIC DROP! Mario Díaz-Balart won the election with 65% of the votes. Annie received 35%.

I will always be grateful for her advice and counsel while I was serving as Executive Director of the Dade Delegation, as it could be overwhelming sometimes. And of course, her friendship.

Keep on being the sparkle, Annie!

FOR US CONGRESS
25th Congressional District

To the Editor
The Miami Herald
One Herald Plaza
Miami, FL 33132

September 30, 2002

Dear Sir:

The US policy on Cuba is very complex and multifaceted. Sometimes, too much emphasis is given to the trade restrictions and not enough to the real problem, which is the oppression of the Cuban people by the Castro regime. People who live on the island have their human rights systematically denied every day; they cannot speak freely, they cannot travel freely inside and/or outside of their country. Dissidents are unjustly persecuted, jailed and even tortured for the simple reason that they express their opposition to the government. I am a widow of a Bay of Pigs veteran; as such, I fully understand the pain of oppressed people.

The Castro regime has ruled Cuba for over 43 years without holding a free and democratic election, and political parties other than the official Communist party, are outlawed. Unfortunately, the 40-year-old US economic policy on Cuba has failed miserably to change this. Up to now, the Cuban-American congressional delegation has been unwilling to take a leadership role in exploring alternatives to a policy that has not been successful, and that in all likelihood has been counter-productive.

As a U.S. Congresswoman, I will not be afraid to take the first steps to make a change to this policy by considering different options, and working with my colleagues in Congress to build consensus. Even former supporters of our current policy, such as Republican US House Majority Leader Dick Armey, realize that we need to take a different path to help the Cuban people and change is imminent. While I served on the Committee of Economic Development and International Trade in the Florida House of Representatives, a study was conducted to determine the impact of future commerce between Florida and a free Cuba. The study found that Florida would benefit from open trade, and it would stimulate our economy. I will fight to bring new economic choices to South Florida without compromising the human rights of the Cuban people.

As Americans, our freedom to travel to Cuba is limited by special interests, which do not believe that true democracy can result from a free exchange of ideas and culture between our two countries. The current outdated policy has only served to isolate the Cuban people, and has given the Castro regime an excuse for their failed economic policies. Paradoxically, some of the same people who strongly voice their disapproval of changing the US policy on Cuba, have sent over $8 billion to their relatives and friends, and also travel to Cuba regularly both through the legal route, or through third countries.

It is time to frame a changed posture towards Cuba; one that doesn't pander to the Cuban regime but likewise, doesn't punish the Cuban people. It is time to put an end to the tired and fruitless formulas that have helped perpetuate the power of a tyrant. It is time to take a strong leadership stand on the US Policy on Cuba, and consider an effective policy alternative that will help the Cuban people and the people of Florida. It is time to send a leader to Congress who will provide South Floridians with an effective voice to represent them. I am that leader.

Sincerely,

Annie Betancourt
Candidate For US
25 Congressional District

P.O. Box 163906 • Snapper Creek Branch • Miami, FL 33116-9998
Phone (305) 596-2435 • Fax (305) 596-4702

THE DÍAZ-BALART FAMILY

The Díaz-Balart family has been in the business of public service for almost 100 years, since Rafael José Díaz-Balart became a municipal judge in the city of Palma Soriano, Cuba, in the early 1930s. He served as City Council President and Mayor of Banes (a municipality located on the eastern part of Cuba) and went on to serve in the Cuban House of Representatives.

Rafael's son and namesake, whom he practiced law within Havana, served as the Majority Leader of the House of Representatives under Fulgencio Batista's regime and also served in the Cuban Senate. In 1959, he went into exile in the United States during the Cuban Revolution.

On February 10, 2007, Florida International University (FIU) dedicated the Rafael Díaz-Balart Hall as the building housing the FIU College of Law.

LINCOLN AND MARIO DÍAZ-BALART

Lincoln Díaz-Balart (LDB) served as a member of the Florida Legislature (House and Senate) from 1986 to 1992, when he was elected to the United States House of Representatives. LDB faithfully served in Congress until 2011, when he chose to retire. His younger brother, Mario, also served in the Florida Legislature (House, Senate, and House again) from 1988 to 2002. Since 2003, Mario has served in Congress as a Member of the House of Representatives.

I first met Lincoln and Mario during the 1989 session. I was working for State Representative Nilo Juri (R-Hialeah) and the three of them shared a townhouse in Tallahassee during that session. Knowing Lincoln and Nilo, it would have been a treat to be a fly on the wall when they were roommates, because they could not be more opposite.

Over the years, we continued to work together, and our friendship continued to grow. For the last 12 years, my wife has worked with the Diaz-Balart brothers as president and CEO of the Congressional Hispanic Leadership Institute (CHLI), which Lincoln and Mario co-founded along with Ileana Ros-Lehtinen.

In 2018, while serving as Chair of the Greater Miami Chamber of Commerce, we honored Ileana Ros-Lehtinen with the Chamber's inaugural Mary Brickell Award. As part of the awards ceremony, I asked Lincoln to have a "fireside chat" with Ileana, while almost 500 chamber members joined as part of the monthly Trustee luncheons. It was a very special moment for all those in attendance. For months afterwards, members were still talking about the luncheon!

The public servant mantle continues with Lincoln's son, Daniel, a former prosecutor (Assistant State Attorney) with the Miami-Dade State Attorney's Office.

There's obviously so much more I can share about Lincoln and Mario given our 30+ year friendship. I am so pleased and honored that Lincoln accepted my invitation to participate in this book, in his own words. Gracias Lincoln!

L-R: Daniel, Jose and Lincoln Díaz-Balart, me and Congressman Mario Díaz-Balart. (Photo courtesy of the South Florida Hispanic Chamber of Commerce.)

MIGUEL DE GRANDY

I first met Miguel in the summer of 1988 when he was running in the Republic primary for the state house district 111. I don't remember who introduced us or how we met, it could have been some trial lawyer friends.

Miguel is probably the smartest boss I've ever had. At 22, he obtained his jurist doctorate degree from the University of Florida, College of Law. Miguel began his legal and public service career in 1981 as an Assistant State Attorney, in Miami-Dade County. After leaving the State Attorney's office, he founded a law firm.

During the 1988 Florida Republican primary, his opponent was a Cuban American realtor named Carlos Valdez. He always wore a perfectly pressed suit, shirt, and tie. He drove a Mercedes-Benz and always wore a two-toned Rolex. Valdez beat us by two or three votes after two recounts.

After the election was over, Miguel and I went our separate ways, but I made sure to stay in contact with him. We got along well, and I enjoyed getting to know his (first) wife and mom during the election.

In politics, in particular when you are young, it's important to work for elected officials who have a great reputation or brand, as it will stay with you for a very long time. It is like getting in on the ground floor of a 20-story condo building. If you buy early, you'll have lots of equity when it's time to sell. I mean that in the nicest and most flattering way.

In the summer of 1989, U.S. Representative Claude Pepper died unexpectedly. Pepper had been in public service, off and on, since 1929 when he served in the Florida House of Representatives. His death would alter Miami's political landscape for decades to come. Ileana Ros-Lehtinen would become the first Latina elected to Congress. Lincoln "replaced" Ileana in the Florida Senate, and Miguel de Grandy "replaced" Lincoln in the Florida House of Representatives. We worked just as hard that second campaign and upon Miguel's election, he hired me as his Legislative Aide.

A HISTORIC LEGACY

Although Miguel only served five years in the legislature, from 1989 to 2004, he left an incredible legacy including a Breastfeeding law, several reapportionment cases which lead to the election of the first African American woman (Carrie Meek) since Florida's reconstruction, and the first Hispanic woman (Ileana Ros-Lehtinen) to Congress (from Florida), to ensuring reparations for African Americans via a Claims Bill.

To me, the Claims Bill is his most significant work. The community and African American legislators had been seeking reparations for many years, but the Bill always failed.

The Rosewood Bill (House Bill 591), and what it stands for, is so powerful that it was made into a movie (1997) called Rosewood directed by John Singleton. Florida's consideration of a bill to compensate victims of racial violence was the first by any U.S. state. In January 2023, the town celebrated the 100 anniversary of the *Rosewood* massacre, which led to the destruction of a black town in 1923.

The Florida Black Caucus recognized Miguel's efforts by making him an honorary member of their Caucus.

I am so honored to have worked for someone like Miguel, who recognized such a horrific wrong, and against all odds, beat the system.

ALEXANDER PENELAS

"One of the other candidates in this race became in 2000 the single most treacherous and dishonest person I dealt with during the campaign anywhere in America," stated Vice President Al Gore in a Miami Herald article during the 2000 election, indirectly referring to Alex Penelas, and praising his opponent, U.S. Rep. Peter Deutsch. Both democrats were running for the U.S. Senate.

I first met Alex in 1990 when he was running for county commission. I was working for State Representative Miguel de Grandy as his legislative aide, and the districts overlapped significantly, which meant we had the same voters and their information. With Miguel's blessing, I worked on Alex's campaign and got to know him well. As a result, we developed a wonderful friendship. He is someone that I've come to admire tremendously over the years.

Alex grew up in the most Cuban of Cuban cities—Hialeah, Florida, whose Cuban American population stands at 73% (as of the 2020 Census). It was higher when Alex first was elected. Alex's father was an anti-communist Cuban labor leader who was condemned to death by Castro. His dad sought sanctuary at the Costa Rican embassy in Havana as Penelas' mother and two older brothers fled to Miami. In 1961, his father joined them in Miami, where Penelas was born later that year.

Alex recounts that: "I was actually a promise because they didn't think they'd see each other again—if in fact they did, they'd have another child."

Once in the U.S., his parents purchased a house for $17K. He remembers his father telling him that, "If I had $1,000 at the time, and bought 10 homes, we would've been set for life." His father worked various jobs, including as a tomato picker and hotel waiter. His mother Mirta worked as a seamstress and hotel housekeeper.

During the campaign, I had the opportunity to work with his mom and, let me tell you, she was fearless and super politically savvy. The woman understood retail politics better than most politicians. Every candidate should wish for and needs a "Mirta" in their corner. Rest in peace, Mirta Penelas.

Like a lot of Cubans, Alex is a local boy when it comes to his education. He studied political science at Biscayne College (now St. Thomas University) and received his law degree from the University of Miami in 1985. At 25, he won a seat on the Hialeah City Council, making history as the youngest member ever. He served from 1987 to 1990. History repeated itself in 1990 when he was elected to the Dade County Commission as its youngest member, defeating an incumbent, Cuban American Jorge Valdez.

On October 1, 1996, Penelas makes history again becoming the Mayor of Dade County (renamed Miami-Dade County in 1997), a first for a Cuban American.

Alex stood out in Miami politics being young, talented, good-looking, charismatic, and a registered Democrat. People magazine named him "Sexiest Politician" in 1999. Nice!

ELIÁN GONZALEZ

It was Thanksgiving weekend, 1999, when Elián Gonzalez, a five-year-old Cuban boy, was found by two anglers, floating in a tube a few miles off Fort Lauderdale's coast. The Cuban community considered it a miracle and demanded that the boy stay in the U.S. His father, back in Cuba, and Fidel Castro asked for his return.

The fight—keep Elián in the United States with his family and honor is mother's wishes, or send him back to a Communist Cuba, to live with his father—would go on for months, make international news, produce hundreds of protests in the streets of Little Havana, and ultimately force President Clinton and Attorney General Janet Reno to act, which they did, by taking the child by force in the early morning hours.

No matter how many times I've seen that iconic photo, I still have a difficult time not crying. He was five years old. I was five years old when I came to this country, with my parents. I can't image facing what he did at five years old.

(Photo Credit: Alan Díaz/Associated Press)

In my opinion, the Elián saga also ended Alex Penelas' chances of getting elected to a state-wide or national office, either appointment or by election, because he refused to cooperate with the Clinton Administration or with the police, who were dressed in commando uniforms and brandishing assault weapons, on the morning they took Elián. Furthermore, the Elián saga has been credited with some Cuban American voters walking away from the Democratic party and possibly costing Al Gore Florida (2000 election). After two recounts, Gore lost Florida by 537 votes, out of the 6 million casts.

Fast forward to 2004, Alex is hoping to replace Bob Graham as Florida's next United States Senator and the first Cuban American in the U.S. Senate. The national Democrats shut him down. He came in third. According to several news articles, "Some party loyalists hadn't forgiven him for his criticism of the Clinton administration's handling of Elián

Gonzalez, and for what they perceived as Penelas' tepid support of Al Gore during the 2000 presidential campaign."

At the age of 43 and having been in office since 1987, Alex "walked away from politics" and threw himself into fatherhood, launched a career in real estate, staying out of the political spotlight for 15 years until he announced in October of 2019 that he would run again for his old job as Miami-Dade mayor.

In my opinion, Gore did not remember that you never forget nor betray the people who elected you. *"You dance with the one that brung you,"* as President Reagan would often say. You stand by them as faithfully as they have stood by you. That's what Alex did. He did the right and just thing (standing by the Cuban community).

In politics, like in life, you never know what's around the corner that will be great or knock you out of the game. For Alex Penelas, that knockout punch metaphorically came from the saga of a five-year-old Cuban boy named Elián Gonzalez.

SPRING OF 1992: PRESIDENTIAL PRIMARIES

I was living in Tallahassee and looking for a high-profile job in Governor Lawton Childs' Administration. As a registered Republican, it was an uphill battle, so I changed my party registration. What I remember about Alex was how helpful he was to me during that job search. Whenever Alex visited Tally, he would make sure we would meet, and he'd take me around to meet Cabinet members, elected officials, and political operatives. He sang my praises and pushed my candidacy.

The kind of loyalty and friendship he demonstrated is unique and I will always be forever grateful to him. In the end, unfortunately, nothing panned out job wise, and that's okay. Most importantly, Alex went above and beyond to help me. For me, loyalty is the most important factor in politics, and in life.

As I reflect on my time in Tallahassee, those twelve years (1988-2000) taught me some incredible and valuable lessons, personal and professional. It cemented what would become life-long friendships. I gained a first-rate education on the inner working of government by being part of it. I learned how to be a great legislative aide and public servant.

I would also feel the sting of sexual harassment, racism, racist situations, and work with elected and appointed officials who had a tough time controlling their alcohol and "recreational" drug use habits. And a few, unfortunately, elected officials and legislative staffers, ended up serving time in jail or prison. Careers they had worked so hard to achieve, down the drain, for a failure of moral and ethical leadership.

I can tell you that I am a better person today because of those experiences, the good and the bad. I have tried to pass my wisdom on to as many young people involved in politics as I can, in hopes they can avoid some of the traps and reach success at a much faster rate than I did. And most importantly, stay out of "bad" trouble.

In the end, I would not trade any of the experiences and my time as a political operative or legislative aide for anything in the world. Politics, after all these years, still gets me giddy and excited.

Chapter 9

TALL TALES FROM TALLAHASSEE

As you may imagine, there are dozens of stories that I could share about the Tallahassee culture, the legislative process, and all the diverse and interesting people I met. For this book, I've chosen some interesting, PG rated stories that I hope you'll appreciate reading about and learning from.

The first story is the most important one. Why? Because from my point of view, it really sets up how Cuban Americans gained power in Tallahassee. What happened at the state Capitol in the fall of 1988 no doubt reverberated at the local and national level.

WHEN IS A BETRAYAL, NOT A BETRAYAL?

Politically speaking, for the Cuban Americans in the Florida Legislature, in my opinion, the election of State Representative Tom Gustafson (D-Broward) as Speaker of the Florida House in 1988 was the most pivotal moment these Cuban American legislators had faced in Tallahassee.

For some background, the 1998 general election brought additional Cuban Americans to the Florida House. George H. W. Bush was elected President of the United States after an 8-year run as President Ronald Reagan's Vice President.

In Florida, although the legislature was still in the hands of Democrats, there was a shift in the air; the state was becoming more conservative, more Red. And in fact, the Florida Senate split evenly after the 2000 general election: 20 Democrats and 20 Republicans.

In 1988, prior to the general election, there were seven Cuban Americans in the Florida House of Representatives:

- Alberto "Al" Gutman (R-Miami)
- Luis C. Morse (R-Little Havana)
- Lincoln Díaz-Balart (R-Miami)
- Mario Díaz-Balart (R-Miami)
- Nilo Juri (R-Hialeah)
- Luis Rojas (R-Hialeah)
- Carlos Valdez (R-West Miami)

In the summer before the 1988 November general election, there was an attempt by some conservative Democrats, led by Rep. Carl Carpenter (D-Plant City), to join forces with some moderate Republicans and steal the Speakership from Gustafson, who claimed to have the 68+ Democrat votes he needs. Dale Patchett (R-Vero Beach), the House Minority Leader at the time, said the GOP could work out a deal with Carpenter.

Unbeknownst to Representatives Carpenter and Patchett, the Cuban Americans did not want to betray the Grand Old Party (GOP) and vote for a Democrat for Speaker, no matter how conservative he was. And this was decided at a late-night meeting, on Election night, with Gustafson himself.

Here's the brilliant part: the Cuban Americans worked out a deal with Gustafson to gain seats on the House Appropriations committee, on other committees as Vice Chairs, and having their own Caucus office, just like the African American members had. The icing on the cake was a promise by Gustafson that he would support the various projects the seven Cuban American legislators might want included in the state's budget; and give them advice regarding how they might better navigate the appropriations process as a group.

Once this came to light, the Florida GOP party leaders were furious with the Cuban Americans. Can you blame them? I once read a quote that has always stuck, "Power is not given, it is taken." This would be the case here. The way they (GOP leaders) saw it was if the seven Cubans had voted with the GOP and Carpenter's group – AND NOT BETRAYED THEM – the GOP and Dale Patchett would have had de facto "control" of the Florida House for the first time in years. One GOP member quoted in the Orlando Sentinel said: "For the first time, we would have gone from the doghouse to the penthouse."

My friend Lincoln Díaz-Balart, one of the Cuban legislators at the time shared with me that the Cuban Caucus trusted and admired Gustafson. Not so when it came to the GOP leadership. According to a story from the Orlando Sentinel, "The Cuban Americans did not believe an alliance with Carpenter would help their constituents. Equally important, Carpenter's good-old-boy style did not translate well with the Hispanics, whose ears are sensitive to Anglo crudities, real or imagined."

In 1988, Cubans were still relatively "new" to Tallahassee. It wasn't unusual to hear whispers about us in the hallways, mispronunciation of our names, and sometimes straight-out racism. The first time I experienced racism was in Tallahassee during a Legislative Session. I now realize how fortunate I was that this was the first time. The Cuban American legislators also knew their numbers in the House would increase along with Miami-Dade County's population. When you have the numbers on your side, it's hard to lose.

Ultimately, you can say that the Cuban American legislators outsmarted the GOP establishment by NOT BETRAYING them and because of it, got a hell of a deal for their respective districts and Miami-Dade County, thus securing their power in the Florida Legislature for years to come. It would be 1998 before the executive and legislative branches would be in hands of Republicans.

After his two-year term, in 1990, Speaker Gustafson was the running mate of Bill Nelson, who ran for governor that year but lost the Democratic primary to Senator Lawton Chiles, who would go on to defeat Republican Gov. Bob Martinez. (Source: Tampa Bay Times; Steve Bousquet). After the defeat in 1990, Gustafson didn't seek statewide office, a congressional seat, or major appointment during President Clinton's term in office, that I can recall. It was not until 2012 that Gustafson ran again for public office, and unfortunately he lost.

Speaker Tom Gustafson (standing) circa 1988 or 1989.

THE WREATH: HIALEAH POLITICS 101

In February of 1989, I went to work for Nilo Juri (R-Hialeah), a freshman Florida State Representative. I wanted to desperately work for a state representative as a legislative aide. To me, working for a State Representative as a legislative aide would give my fledgling political career a huge boost. It would give me access to powerful and influential individuals, both in the private and public sectors. In politics, Access = Success. It's not what you know, but WHO you know. That was certainly the way it worked 30 plus years ago.

Rep. Nilo Juri (R-Hialeah)

Between February and June, I got to know Nilo well. I realized what a good-hearted guy he was. He was smart, loved his wife and two daughters. He loved helping people. He ran a successful textile business. He was Cuban Lebanese which is quite the combo when it comes to cooking food. This was the first time that I had middle eastern food and it was delicious. Think couscous, labneh, hummus, pita bread ... okay, I am getting hungry! As I think back about Nilo's cooking, it is the first time that the concept of "food bringing people together" clicked with me. Why? Because it was not unusual for the Jewish members of the legislature, as well as other members, to stop by Nilo's office to join him in a quick meal. Food allowed him to make new friends, and quickly.

NILO'S OBSESSION

We all have our faults, no one is perfect, as the saying goes. Nilo's obsession was being mayor of the City of Hialeah by beating (electorally of course) Raul Martinez, the city's first Cuban mayor and one of the few Cuban Democrats elected to public office. Nilo subscribed to the philosophy that if you try and try again, you will succeed. When it was all said and done, Nilo had run for mayor of Hialeah five times, losing each time to the incumbent Raul Martinez. He came "close" (not really) in 1993, losing by 273 votes.

In the end, Raul served for 24 years as Mayor of Hialeah. That, in spite of being indicted and going through three jury trials, he is a Cuban "Teflon" man, meaning nothing sticks to him.

In his obsession about being mayor of Hialeah, Nilo spent a lot of time during the 1989 legislative session plotting for his next campaign for mayor of Hialeah. In fact, he did not finish his term in the Legislature, which would have ended in November of 1990. He resigned in the summer of 1989 so that he could meet the filing deadline for the Hialeah mayor's race.

I met Raul Martinez a few times, but I don't know him. We have mutual friends and colleagues in common, and I was not tainted by Nilo's views or what he thought of Raul. What I can say is at the time, Raul came across very self-assured. He was the "King of Hialeah"—a town that at one point was 90% Cuban American – according to the U.S. Census. My guess is Raul didn't think much of Nilo and his political ban of brothers, and that he enjoyed beating Nilo at the ballot box come election time. He did it five times.

Being a legislative aide gave me entry into Florida and Miami politics. I was part of a "club" of young Cuban American political operatives going to Tallahassee, a band of brothers and sisters who liked each other and we all worked well with each other ... the majority of the time.

The legislative session in Florida is 60 days, assuming it adjourns on time. In 1989, we started in April and finished in May or early June. During the last few week of session, it gets intense. The workday starts at 7:30 am and you could be at your desk past 10:00 pm. Everyone is up in Tallahassee making sure their legislation either gets passed or amended or killed. It really feels like Miami International Airport at Christmas time. If you've never experienced it, you should!

I think it was during this crazy time, Mayor Raul Martinez, who was president of the Florida League of Cities decided to visit Tallahassee. He and the House Majority Leader were friendly, having agreed to exchange "jobs for a day" and so Mayor Martinez is seated on the house floor. Nilo, who is also on the floor of the House, gets wind of this and makes a point of order.

A point of order, according to govinfo.gov, "Calls upon the chair (in this case, the Speaker of the Florida House) to make a ruling. The chair may rule on the point of order or submit it to the judgment of the assembly. If the chair accepts the point of order, it is said to be ruled 'well taken.' If not, it is said to be ruled "not well taken.'"

Once recognized by the Speaker, Nilo reads from the House Rules where it states lobbyists are prohibited on the House Floor. Raul is a registered lobbyist for the Florida League of Cities and probably for the City of Hialeah, so technically, he is a lobbyist. A few moments after Nilo's remarks, Mayor Raul Martinez is escorted off the House Floor.

Wow! How embarrassing! Here is the Mayor of Hialeah, one of Florida's largest cities, Nilo's hometown, president of the Florida League of Cities, and at the time, the Democrat's best hope of electing a Cuban American to congress, being escorted off the House floor.

There was a lot of excitement in our office over the next 48 hours. The next day, at our Capitol office, we received a black wreath. At first, I didn't make the connection. As I said before, I was so naïve back them. I thought it had been delivered by mistake. I felt sorry for whoever had passed away. If I remember correctly, Nilo took the wreath as a death threat and he had me call both Capitol police and the Florida Department of Law Enforcement.

The investigation discovered that a young lady—a friend of Raul, and also a friend of mine—had paid cash at a local florist just a block from the Capitol for the wreath. When asked by law enforcement if he wanted to prosecute her, he said no. I am not sure why, we never discussed it.

After the legislation session, Nilo announced his intentions to run for Mayor of Hialeah. I told Nilo I was not interested in "Hialeah politics" and would be resigning soon.

Former Hialeah Mayor Raul Martinez.

Photo of the Doyle Floral shop where the wreath was bought.

For most of its time as a city, Hialeah has had one state senator and two state representatives represent it in Tallahassee. The state senator and one state representative have always aligned with Martinez. Nilo was the odd man out. I lost touch with Nilo as he continued to run for mayor of Hialeah. In the end, Nilo's obsession with being mayor of Hialeah got the best of him.

Fast forward a few years later, in September of 2004, according to a *Sun Sentinel* news story:

> Nilo Juri, the one-time Hialeah mayoral candidate who accused his opponent of voter fraud in 1993, was himself arrested for the same charge on Friday, state and Miami-Dade County investigators said.
>
> According to an arrest affidavit, Juri allegedly had an employee, an acquaintance and his daughter make campaign contributions to a county commission candidate and three Hialeah commission candidates. He told investigators he wanted to gain influence for a planned campaign for Hialeah mayor in 2005.
>
> More than a decade ago in 1993, Juri was the losing candidate in a Hialeah mayoral race, won by longtime mayor Raul Martinez. Juri subsequently alleged absentee voter fraud by his opponent and won a civil case against Martinez but lost during a rematch.
>
> On Friday, Miami-Dade prosecutors charged Juri with five felony counts of making contributions in the name of another, one felony count of exceeding campaign contribution limitations, and four misdemeanor counts of exceeding limitations on contributions.

For this book, I reconnect with Nilo recently after 30 plus years since working with him. He left Hialeah and relocated to South Dade where he currently resides.

I am so thankful that Nilo gave me my first break, allowing me to become a legislative aide to a Member of the Florida Legislature at the age of 22. Today, I see 22-year-olds running all over Washington, with no clue as to what they want to do, and I think how blessed I was that at that age, I was on a path to reach success and surpass my parent's wishes for me—to have the best life possible. A life a Communist Cuba would never give me.

Chapter 10
IN THEIR OWN WORDS

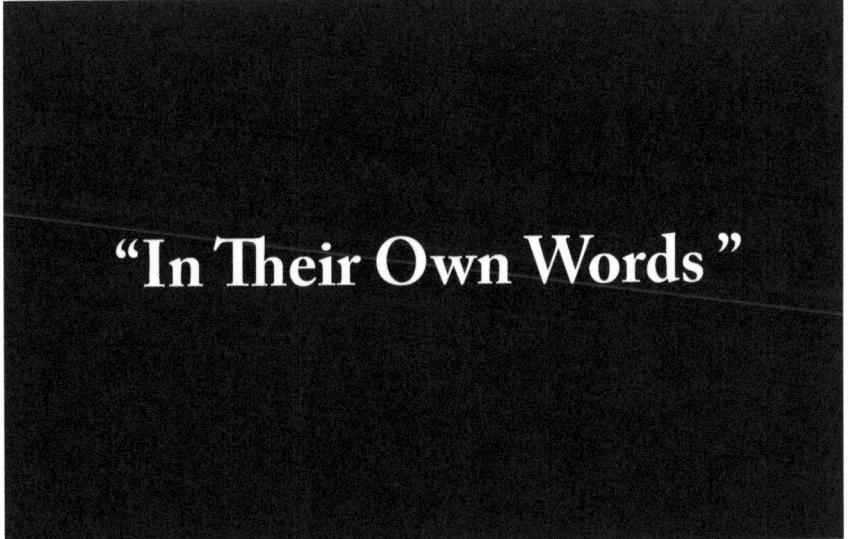

"In Their Own Words"

I n thinking about this book and what to include, what to leave out, I really wanted you to hear directly from some of the individuals who were the history makers. Those that were the first, those that blazed the trail for others, and to hear from a beneficiary of the trailblazers.

It is also important to hear from non-Cuban Americans who were there as Cuban Americans gained more and more political clout, and how they worked with Cuban Americans. In addition to Ileana Ros-Lehtinen and Lincoln Díaz-Balart, I am humbled and honored that

Congresswoman Debbie Wasserman Schultz (D-FL), David Lawrence, former Publisher (1989-1999), *The Miami Herald,* and Florida House of Representatives Speaker-Designate Daniel Perez, a Republican, Cuban American from Miami are sharing their thoughts and perspectives with you.

Debbie had front row seats and worked closely with most of the first Cuban Americans, first in Tallahassee and later in Congress.

David Lawrence's perspective is a bit different than that of Debbie's. His front row seat was as publisher of Miami's hometown newspaper, a paper not liked by the majority/most/many of Cuban Americans before and while he was publisher. *The Miami Herald* and Miami's Cuban American community have had a love-hate relationship since the late 1970s/early 1980s. I am not sure if that is the case today, and I give credit to David for bridging that divide. Alberto Ibargüen, who David hired and replaced him as editor and publisher, also should get some credit. And so should the Cuban American community, who I believe has matured over the decades.

As for Speaker-Designate Perez, a beneficiary of the legacies laid by Ileana and Lincoln, and a trailblazer in his own right, it's all about the future.

ABOUT LINCOLN DÍAZ-BALART

Born in Havana, Cuba, into a family of public servants since the 1930s, Díaz-Balart is a lawyer by trade. And a damn good one!

In 1986, he was elected to serve in the Florida House of Representatives. In 1989, during a special election held due to the death of Florida Congressman Clause Pepper (D-FL), he was elected to the Florida Senate where he served until his election to Congress in 1992. Díaz-Balart served in congress until his retirement in 2011. He was succeeded by his brother, Mario Díaz-Balart, who was already a member of Congress representing an adjacent district.

BELOW IS MY INTERVIEW WITH LDB:

CFO: What legislative achievement in Congress are you most proud of and why?

LDB: Gracias, Carlos. The Nicaraguan Adjustment and Central American Relief Act (known by its initials as NACARA), which became law in 1997. Let me share with you part of my upcoming book:

In 1996, Congress had passed a law, authored by Rep. Lamar Smith of Texas, ending the possibility of "Suspension of Deportation." As a result, it became extremely difficult for undocumented immigrants to legalize their status.

The anguish of tens of thousands of Nicaraguans in South Florida was increasing daily as the Nicaraguan Review Program neared its expiration date: June 12, 1997. I was in constant contact with many, and I felt their anguish.

In passing NACARA in November of 1997, every Nicaraguan in the United States who had arrived before December 31, 1995, would receive Permanent Legal Residency (and, thus, be eligible for U.S. citizenship after 5 years).

Additionally, members of the "ABC Class" plus approximately 30,000 Eastern Europeans, would be eligible for Suspension of Deportation as well.

Here's the interesting thing, NACARA was not passed as an amendment or legislation. It was inserted in the "conference committee" stage of the District of Columbia Appropriations Act of 1998. In hindsight, had it been passed as a bill, President Clinton would have, in all likelihood, vetoed it.

Side note from Carlos: Based on the successful passage of the NACARA Act, in 1998, Congresswoman Carrie Meek and Congressman Alcee Hastings, both from South Florida, asked Lincoln to help them pass the Haitian Refugee Immigration Fairness Act (HRIFA), which was modeled after NACARA.

LDB was a co-sponsor of the bill and as a result, approximately 50,000 Haitians were able to become U.S. legal permanent residents, and ultimately, U.S. citizens.

Miami's Haitian community reminds me of the Cuban community

in many ways. They are a vibrant part of South Florida, they are artists, educators, and entrepreneurs. Most of all, like Cubans, they love and want democracy for their beloved island. Today, several Haitian Americans are serving in local elected offices, as city commissioners, and mayors, and in the Florida Legislature.

CFO: I am hopeful that your son Daniel, in his lifetime, along with his generation, will see a free and democratic Cuba. What are your thoughts on that?

LDB: *My life's constant longing, and a great motivator for action, has been Cuba's freedom. I have always tried to do everything within my power to contribute to keeping the flame of the Cuban nation alive. More than sixty-five years of totalitarianism, destruction, degradation, death, and exile has done indescribable damage to the Cuban nation. But Cuba, while deeply wounded, is not dead.*

Since the days of my early youth, I have been in awe of the ultimate sacrifice made by the patriots who made the Republic of Cuba possible. And I admire all those who have sacrificed, often risking their lives—and even their families' lives—fighting the military dictatorship that has tortured the Cuban nation. The victims of the regime's terror—all of them—are always in my thoughts and in my heart.

Yes, my son Daniel and my grandsons, Lincoln and Edwin, will see Cuba free. On July 11th, 2021, the Cuban people let the world know how it thinks. The people want freedom. The regime's brutal repression avoided—for now—the dream of liberty from becoming a reality. Countless patriots continue to suffer in the tyranny's dungeons, including my admired friend Felix Navarro, his heroine daughter Sailí, and icons of the fight for liberty like Luis Manuel Otero Alcantara and Jose Daniel Ferrer. Heroes of all ages, while the world remains silent. The condemnable lack of solidarity of the international community with Cuba's political prisoners and the Cuban people's right to freedom, continue to be the primary cause for the permanence of the feudal tyranny of the Castro family and their henchmen, but Cuba's freedom is inevitable.

The special relationship that Cuba will develop with the United States will be key to its economic development. Prosperous and democratic Cuba will attract hard-working, talented young people in search of a better future from throughout the world. Orderly and well-planned immigration will help to reinvigorate Cuba and save the nation, when combined with the extraordinary hard work that characterizes Cubans, and the talent and drive that will be provided by new generations of Cuban Americans who will discover their roots in Cuba with love, and who will help to make the second Republic even more prosperous than the first Republic was.

CFO: We are now into what I call the third wave of Cuban Americans serving in public office at the local, state and federal levels. What is your hope for this and the fourth wave? What advice would you share with them?

LDB: *There is no more satisfying human endeavor than public service. Still, almost thirty years later, I am thanked at least monthly by beneficiaries (and their families) of NACARA, a law I authored in 1997, which saved from deportation approximately a half million Nicaraguans, Salvadoreans, Guatemalans, Cubans, and Eastern Europeans. They are hardworking, productive U.S. citizens now. The satisfaction I receive from my public service is my treasure. As Jesus said, "There where you have your treasure, your heart shall be also." What we must avoid is electing public officials whose treasure is in pecuniary gain from public office. Our community must guard against that. It is absolutely fundamental.*

Recently, former Congressman Lincoln Díaz-Balart stepped down as Chair of the Board of Directors of the Congressional Hispanic Leadership Institute (CHLI), a leadership development organization he co-founded with this brother, Congressman Mario Díaz-Balart and former Congresswoman Ileana Ros-Lehtinen, in 2003. To learn more about CHLI, visit www.chli.org. Since 2011, my wife, Mary Ann Gomez has been the organization's CEO.

ABOUT DAVID LAWRENCE, JR.

A New Yorker by birth, David has been a Floridian since 1956. He is a graduate of the University of Florida (Go Gators!). He is a "newsman" at heart, working for seven newspapers over a career that spanned 35 years. From 1989 to 1999, David was Publisher of the Miami Herald, his last newspaper assignment at Knight-Ridder. While at the Herald, the paper won five Pulitzer Prizes!

Since 2000, David has worked in the area of early childhood development and readiness, and currently serves as the chair of The Children's Movement of Florida. He is one of the hardest working "retired" persons I know. Between 1989 and 1997, I had the opportunity to work with and interact with David and some of the Herald's top political reporters and executives. In particular, while I was executive director of the Miami-Dade Delegation.

Every year during Florida's legislative session, the Miami Herald would host a meal function (usually a lunch or dinner) for the members of the Dade Delegation. It was a great opportunity for the legislators to deal directly with the Herald's publisher and top executives, and I assume it was a similar experience for the Herald execs and reporters.

BELOW IS MY INTERVIEW WITH DAVID LAWRENCE:

CFO: David, thank you for welcoming me to your home and for being part of the book. I am honored by it.

Prior to Miami, you were the Editor and Publisher of the *Detroit Free Press* for several years. Two very different communities. While in Detroit, you knew your next assignment would be Miami, and that some, many, certainly a large percentage of the Cuban American community, did not like *The Miami Herald*. Knowing this, what did you do to prepare for it?

DL: *Six months prior, at 47 years old, I started learning Spanish. I hired a tutor in Detroit and hired a tutor once we relocated to Miami. I spent a few weeks in Uruguay where they mostly speak Spanish, versus other South American countries where English was almost a second language. I also read several books about Miami. Lastly, I had access to The Miami Herald and El Nuevo Herald while in Detroit, so I had a pretty idea of what was taking place.*

I felt that if I was going to be responsible for El Nuevo Herald, I needed to speak Spanish.

CFO: Well prepared for sure. I am not surprised. Ok, so now you are in Miami. Tell me about those first few months.

DL: *During the first few months, I spent a lot of time meeting with various community leaders. Alva Chapman, who had spent almost 30 years at the Miami Herald, and retired as Chairman and CEO of Knight-Ridder, handed me a list of 50 people I needed to meet with. I met all of them. They also suggested others to meet with, and I did that as well.*

That's how I learned that Blacks* and African Americans are not the same (in Miami), the difference between exiles and immigrants amongst the Cuban American community; about Miami's Jewish community, and so forth.

*I want to clarify David's response. If you are not familiar with Miami-Dade County's Black/African American community, his response would not make sense. Miami has a wonderful and incredibly diverse African American community, which includes individuals of Bahamian, Haitian, and Jamaican ancestry and heritage. And of course, there African Americans who have been in Florida for generations.

CFO: Let's turn now to the Cuban community's love/hate relationship with its hometown newspaper, The Miami Herald.

DL: *When I took over the Herald, it was still a powerful force in the community. Some called it "The Monster on the Bay." As I came to understand, Jorge Mas Canosa, who at the time was the Chair of the Cuban American National Foundation and founder of MasTec, a Fortune 500 company today, had issues with the paper.*

The Miami Herald *ran an editorial, which is perceived by Mas Canosa pro Castro or not tough enough on Castro. He declares a boycott against* The Miami Herald. *There was excrement on our vending machines. I did not accuse Mas Canosa. I do think it was a mistake on his part. He did not come across very "lower case" democratic.* The Washington Post *even ran a story on it.*

CFO: I remember the boycott. There were signs all over town with the words *"Yo no creo en El Herald,"* which translated to *"I don't believe in the Herald."*

It was only after reading your book, *A Dedicated Life* that I realized the high price you paid as the Miami Herald's top executive. Tell me about that experience.

DL: *The FBI came to me during the boycott and said, "You need to be worried about this." I was not particularly scared, because if someone wants to gun you down somewhere, they can do it.*

I remember going to Christmas mass with my family, and I would have armed, plain-clothe police officers with me. My wife Bobbie and I started our cars by remote control (for two and a half years). What we didn't realize for years later, was that the youngest of our five children was terrorized by this and ended up with complex PTSD, which is what her diagnosis is today. It's had a profound effect on her ability to do anything.

CFO: David, I am so sorry this happened to you and your family.

CFO: So how does the story end? Or does it?

DL: *Ultimately, Mas Canosa wants to meet with me, so I go to his home, and we are sitting under a Tiki Hut in the back yard, and fundamentally, with words that were close to this, "Dave, we are both warriors." That is what he tells me.*

That would be his personality. That's how he would see the relationship. I didn't see it that way. He was also upset that I had been named the local convening chair of the Summit of the Americas. Mas Canosa was a singularly powerful human being.

So, after that (our meeting), and the boycott, and the FBI, etc., life sort of went on and some people in the community, including Cuban Americans like Dr. Joe Greer, spoke up, and I am grateful to them for doing so.

CFO: Last question. Did the boycott work? Did circulation decrease as a result of Mas Canosa's efforts? Did the *Miami Herald* lose money?

DL: *I don't remember any slide of any significance in circulation.*

I cannot remember a profound economic impact as a result of the economic boycott. The profound economic impact in the 1990s was as the internet was coming to be, and people are changing their habits. But the boycott itself did not affect the Herald's revenues.

WHO WAS JORGE MAS CANOSA?

Jorge Lincoln Mas Canosa, who passed away on November 24, 1997, was a Cuban-American businessman who founded the Cuban American National Foundation and MasTec, a Fortune 500 company, which today is run by two of his sons.

Mas Canosa is regarded by some in the U.S. as the most powerful lobbyist on Cuban and anti-Castro political positions. He was labeled a "counterrevolutionary" by the Cuban Communist Party.

I had the opportunity to meet Mas Canosa a few times in the early 1990s, usually at political events or at CANF events. His passion for a free Cuba was exceptional! Mas Canosa was also the driving force behind the creation of both Radio Marti and TV Marti and was appointed chairman of the advisory panel by President Ronald Reagan.

A crowd of thousands follow the hearse carrying the body of Cuban exile leader Jorge Mas Canosa. (Photo credit: Roberto Schmidt/AFP via Getty Images)

ABOUT SPEAKER-DESIGNATE DANIEL PEREZ:

On September 18, 2023, State Representative Perez made history: not only as Speaker-Designate of the Florida House, but as the third Cuban American to do so, following in the footsteps of Marco Rubio. He is a lifelong conservative and longtime resident of Westchester, Florida, from the age of six. His deep roots in the district help drive his dedication to giving back and tirelessly serving his constituents.

First elected to the Florida House of Representatives in 2017 during a special election, he has helped champion common sense, conservative public policy that has made Florida a nationwide leader in areas like education, fiscal stability, business climate, and infrastructure. Daniel is active in the community through his volunteer service on numerous organizations and volunteer activities.

Married to his wife Stephanie and the father of their three beautiful children, Camila Lucia, Matias Daniel, and Paulina Andrea. He is a graduate of Florida State University and Loyola University New Orleans College of Law. He is an attorney and currently works for a local healthcare company.

I had the opportunity to interview Speaker-Designate Perez. Here is what he had to say.

CFO: What inspired you to run for office/seek public service?

SD-DP: *I often speak about my love for Miami and being a Miami guy. Growing up in Westchester and attending Christopher Columbus High School played a huge role in who I am today. Experiencing the warmth and vibrancy of this community, I knew this was where I wanted to start a family, give back, and represent the people who mean so much to me.*

I also felt a personal commitment to serve after witnessing the struggles my parents went through to care for my brother Brian, who has a severe developmental disability. Seeing the gaps in support for those with special needs fueled my desire to be a pioneer of change for that population.

CFO: What does the future of Cuban Politics look like in South Florida over the next 10-15 years?

SD-DP: *The future of Cuban politics in Florida is bright. We're seeing a remarkable growth of Cubans in politics not just in our state, but nationwide. It's incredible to see how much we have done with so little; there aren't many of us, but anywhere you go there will be a Cuban in some leadership role.*

Historically, Cubans have spearheaded the conservative movement on behalf of minorities in South Florida. I think in the next 10 to 15 years, we're going to see the Cuban American political leadership bringing in other Hispanic groups—from Mexicans and Nicaraguans to Colombians and others—who will join us because our conservative principles resonate with more and more people each day.

CFO: How long before Florida has a Cuban American in the Governor's Office, as Attorney General, or Agriculture Commissioner?

SD-DP: *Reflecting on the honor of being designated as the next Speaker of the Florida House, recognizing the path set by our first Cuban American Speaker Marco Rubio, is undoubtedly a significant win for the Cuban community. It's a testament to the phenomenal contributions and leadership roles that our community has embraced over the years. I wish I could predict the future, but what I can tell you is that I'm proud to become the third Cuban American Speaker, and with great Cuban leaders in our community I have no doubt that this is just the beginning.*

CFO: While Cuban Americans will be the majority of Hispanics in Miami-Dade County for a while, there are more non-Cuban Americans in South Florida than ever. How do you see the other Latin American communities engaging in politics over the next 10 years?

SD-DP: *The unfortunate spread of socialism has led to immense growth within the conservative movement in Florida, attracting more Latin Americans to the Republican Party. They see our commitment to putting people first by keeping taxes low, keeping Florida open for business, and ensuring our families can grow and thrive in a free state; so, I believe that in the next 20 years we'll see an overwhelming majority of Hispanics registered proudly as Republicans.*

CFO: What do you hope to accomplish as Florida House Speaker during your term (2024-2026)?

SD-DP: *As the future Speaker from Miami, I want to approach my speakership in a unique way that prioritizes our community. Being Speaker means leading the entire chamber and representing the entire state, but one of my main goals is to ensure Miami–Dade is proud of the work we've done and that the changes we've made make their lives better by the time I leave. This is incredibly important to me because Miami is where I call home and I take pride in making it the best place to live, work, and have a family.*

CFO: Is there anything else you would like to share with the readers?

SD-DP: *I want readers to know that I want to hear from them. As a representative government, we need to hear from you and what your priorities are. These days, you can't go too many steps without hearing about problems with property insurance or affordable housing. I want to hear from you, so we can make sure that we are continually improving the lives of those in Miami and all over the state of Florida.*

In November of 2024, Daniel Perez becomes Speaker of the Florida House.

ABOUT ILEANA ROS-LEHTINEN

Upon her election to Congress in 1989, Ileana Ros-Lehtinen (IRL) made history by becoming the first Hispanic woman to serve in the U.S. House of Representatives. She chose not to run for re-election and retired from Congress, after an almost 40-year career.

Ileana is also the first Hispanic woman to serve in the Florida House of Representatives (1982-1986) and in the Florida Senate (1986-1989). She was also the first Republican in the House to support marriage equality.

I began my political career working as an intern for IRL in the spring of 1988 at the age of 21. That one internship completely changed my life. And I am so grateful for it, as it has been a most wonderful and extraordinary life because of it.

BELOW IS MY INTERVIEW WITH IRL:

CFO: So, just like I never thought I would have a career in politics, I never thought I would write a book about politics, yet here we are. What prompted you to seek public service?

IRL: *The needs I saw in our community prompted me to run in 1982 for a seat in the Florida House of Representatives. I owned and operated a small bilingual private school in Hialeah and the parents of my students would resort to me to help them with different issues.*

One day someone suggested I run for office and that way I could help many people. No one in my family had ever been in public office but my dad and I set off to a GOP campaign school and then armed with our wits and a brochure, we followed the campaign school outline and against the odds, I became the first Hispanic woman elected to the Florida House. Four years later, we did it again and won a Florida Senate seat.

Foreign affairs are domestic affairs in my family and in our Cuban exile community, so a run for a seat in the U.S. Congress where I could truly amplify the voices of freedom fighters in Cuba and advocate for sanctions against oppressive regimes everywhere, was very appealing.

CFO: We know how the IRL history making, public servant story ends. Throughout your time in Congress, really in public service, what do you think the voters appreciated about you the most?

IRL: *I think voters remember my work on Foreign policy issues, sanctions against rogue regimes such as Cuba, Venezuela, Nicaragua, and Iran.*
I think they remember "La Loba Feroz" as Castro called me, and I am glad that they remember my tough stands against dictators and bullies. Four decades in public service between the state and federal government, the biggest accomplishment was what I set out to do in 1982—helping thousands of constituents. Helping with immigration and visa issues, Social Security, Veterans, Medicare issues, replacing military medals, bringing families together, helping on a one-on-one basis, which is what I am most proud of my time in public service.

I have no doubt that South Florida voters would have re-elected IRL another four decades if she would have wanted to stay in Congress. She will go down in history as one of the most popular public servants in South Florida. While small in height, her accomplishments are global in nature. She has been a force for greatness when it comes to supporting and defending democracy, she has broken barriers, and truly shown what it is like to be a true public servant. May God continue to bless this most incredible human being.

Dexter Lehtinen, Ileana and her father, Enrique Ros on Election night, August 1989, when she made history as the first Hispanic women elected to Congress. (Photo courtesy of Ros-Lehtinen)

Ros-Lehtinen Chairing the Foreign Affairs Committee, U.S. House of Representatives. She is the first woman to Chair this Committee. (Photo Courtesy of Ros-Lehtinen)

*TV Screenshot of House Speaker Foley Swearing-In Ileana Ros-Lehtinen
(Photos courtesy of IRL.)*

*I am introducing IRL at the Greater Miami Chamber of Commerce's (GMCC)
Monthly Trustee Luncheon where she received the inaugural Mary Brickell Award,
2019. (Photo Source: GMCC)*

ABOUT DEBBIE WASSERMAN SCHULTZ

In 1988, Wasserman Schultz was State Representative Peter Deutsch's legislative aide. Deutsch's district covered mostly Broward County. In 1992, Deutsch successfully ran for Florida's 20th congressional district, and Debbie successfully ran for the State Representative district Deutsch represented in Tallahassee. With her election to the Florida House, at 26, she became the youngest female legislator in the state's history.

Debbie went on to serve eight years in the Florida House until she was termed out. In 2000, Debbie was elected to the Florida State Senate, where she served for four years until being elected to the United States Congress, where she currently serves, representing Florida's 25th district.

In 1998, I worked on my first campaign. From 1989 until 1992, Debbie and I were legislative aides until her election to the Florida House in 1992. Talk about going places and fast. But I don't think any of us legislative aides who worked with her were surprised by her quick rise. You knew she was going places!

I lost touch with her after I relocated to Detroit, Michigan, in 2000. I reconnected with her at a White House Correspondence Dinner in 2006 (and have met since then). It's like we never lost touch, and we spent most of that night catching up.

BELOW IS MY INTERVIEW WITH DWS:

CFO: I would like for you to share with the reader the wonderful relationships you have with the Cuban American legislators, in the Florida House, Florida Senate, and now in Congress?

DWS: *The Florida legislative process is much more congenial. We spend more time together and get to know each other by working closely and in close quarters for concentrated periods of time during the session and Committee weeks. Especially in the Florida Senate with only 40 members, your opportunity to bond with your colleagues is more accessible.*

Before being elected to Congress, I had the opportunity to work closely with Cuban American lawmakers from Florida, such as U.S. Reps. Mario Díaz-Balart and Marco Rubio. Since arriving in Washington, I also worked with icons like Floridian former U.S. Rep. Ileana Ros-Lehtinen, as well as others from across the country, such Rep. Albio Sires, Sen. Bob Menendez, and Rep. Robert Menendez Jr.

My work has focused on the ongoing political and humanitarian crisis facing Cubans, including ensuring that we continue to support access to legitimate information, news, and internet access for Cubans on the Island. I have also targeted my efforts toward demanding accountability for the perpetrators of human rights violations and supporting continued sanctions against the Cuban regime—all of which I am able to work on collaboratively and across the aisle with my Cuban American colleagues in Congress.

Beyond that, I've worked with several Cuban members on issues of concern in the broader region, including the threat posed by authoritarian governments in Venezuela and Nicaragua, security and counter-narcotics cooperation with Caribbean nations, and countering growing Russian and Chinese influence in the Western Hemisphere.

I count on my Cuban colleagues for support and insight in this work.

CFO: Growing up in Miami politics and working with political icons like Elaine Bloom, Jack Gordon, Larry Smith, Sally Heyman, Elaine Gordon, "Uncle Sherman Winn," Gwen Margolis, and you, to name a few, I am fully aware of the Jewish community's political power and influence. Can you share with the reader the relationship between both of our communities and why it is so important to freedom and democracy?

DWS: *The relationship between the Jewish and Cuban communities runs deep, especially in Florida. For decades, the Jewish leadership in Florida at every level has been passionate in pursuing strong working relations with our Cuban brothers and sisters because of our shared values regarding freedom and justice.*

Our state has been a refuge for migrants for generations, from European Jews escaping pogroms and persecution, to Latin Americans fleeing despotism and destitution. My hometown of Weston, and South Florida in general, serve as a living illustration of the ties that bind our communities—our shared histories of resettlement and acclimation, and our shared values of family, faith, and freedom. All of us are shaped by the intergenerational experience of being a stranger in a strange land. All of us are anchored to tragedy and trauma. Many of the challenges our parents and grandparents faced, from terror and tyranny to bias and bigotry, continue to rear their ugly heads.

In the political realm, these common threads have manifested in cooperation on many fronts, from immigration and foreign assistance to fighting bigotry and protecting our democracy. That's part of why I co-founded the Congressional Latino-Jewish Caucus, which is dedicated to enhancing ties between our communities and identifying areas of mutual interest, in service to the promotion of justice and democracy.

CFO: Politically speaking, where do you see South Florida going as it becomes more and more diverse with South and Central Americans, as well as Haitians, moving to South Florida as a result of political unrest in their respective homelands?

DWS: *South Florida has always been shaped by the various diaspora groups that contribute to our culture, community, and our politics—so this is nothing new. My town of Weston, affectionately referred to as "Westonzuela," is a great example here.*

The truth is that people who come here are motivated by the same American Dream that brought my grandparents over, regardless of what pushed them to leave. That universal drive to ensure a better life for your children is what has allowed South Florida to grow throughout the years.

They've experienced firsthand the challenges of our broken immigration system, and they know what it means to leave home and start over because they have seen what happens when democracy and human rights are stripped away by demagogues.

I wouldn't want to generalize the beliefs or values of the most recent cohort of Latin American and Caribbean migrants, but I can tell you without a doubt that they are engaged in politics, news, and the local community.

They do not hesitate to step up and speak out against injustice or contribute to the dialogue, so I am confident that they'll be just as effective in mobilizing politically as the Cuban diaspora has been.

Congresswoman Debbie Wasserman Schultz (D-FL) and me at an annual Congressional Hispanic Caucus Institute (CHCI) Gala Dinner during Hispanic Heritage Month, in Washington, DC at the convention center.

Side Bar: Through the years, I've had close friends of the Jewish faith. After a life changing trip to Israel for a week in 2012, as a guest of the American Jewish Committee, I realized truly realized importance of the close ties between the Cuban community and the Jewish Community.

Chapter 11

THE FUTURE IS BRIGHT AND SUNNY!

For this final chapter, I focus on five important topics that will close out the book:

1. The Rise of Latinas in Florida Politics
2. New Kids on the Block
3. Florida's Shifting Hispanic Demographics
4. The Importance of Bipartisanship
5. Friendship from Across the Aisle

THE RISE OF LATINAS IN FLORIDA POLITICS

In 1982, Ileana Ros-Lehtinen set and raised the bar by being the first Hispanic woman elected to the Florida House of Representatives. She is also the first Hispanic woman elected to the Florida Senate and ultimately, elected the United States House of Representatives. As mentioned previously in the book, Cuban Democrat Rosario Kennedy is a trailblazer. Her election to the City of Miami Commission in 1985 was a defining moment for Miami's Cuban American community and, I believe, for Democrats in general. I

Today, dozens of Cuban American and Latinas have and are serving in public and appointed political office in Miami, Tallahassee, and Washington, D.C. For the Cuban American community, it all started with Rosario and Ileana in my humble opinion.

When it comes to Cuban American and Latina women, the good news is that since 2000, there have been several who have been elected to the Florida Legislature, including:

- Anitere Flores, former State Representatives and State Senator
- Ana Maria Rodriguez, Former State Representative and current State Senator (as of 2023)
- Ana Rivas Logan, former State Representative
- Alexis Calatayud, current State Senator (as of 2023)
- Alina Garcia, current State Representative (as of 2023)
- Ileana Garcia, current State Senator (as of 2023)
- Vicky Lopez, current State Representative (as of 2020)

I am not surprised to see Anitere Flores on that list. Her mom, Ana Maria Monte Flores, a wonderful public servant, would often bring Anitere to work meetings and the halls of government. This was way before we had "Bring Your Daughter to Work" days. Alina Garcia and I served as legislative aides back in the day and became good friends, always getting into some "good trouble" in Tallahassee.

Florida's current Lieutenant Governor, Jeanette Nuñez, is the first Cuban American woman to serve in that role. She also served as a legislative aide, which is how we know each other.

I am most impressed with Florida State Senator Alexis Calatayud. She is a vibrant, passionate young Cuban American and lifelong Republican. She grew up in the State Senate District (38) she currently represents. Her story is one of consistency and commitment. Most recently, she served as the Director of Policy and Programs at the Florida Department of Education (FLDOE).

Prior to her role in Legislative Affairs at FLDOE, Alexis was Representative Vance Aloupis' campaign manager in the 2018 and 2020 election cycles and served as his legislative aide from 2018 to 2020. A graduate of Florida International University (FIU), she served two terms as student body president and a University trustee implementing institutional, local, state, and federal advocacy strategies to advance college affordability efforts while interning for Senator Marco Rubio.

Upon graduating from FIU, she partnered with national non-profit organizations to train Florida student leaders on candidate engagement strategies, in advance of the 2016 campaign cycle to center candidate focus on issues that mattered to students—postsecondary affordability, student loans, and cost of living. Alexis then moved to Washington, D.C., to broaden the scope of this work, developing national student leadership training programs to educate and prepare over 500 college campus presidents to advocate for their student body and local community on federal, state, and institutional issues. (Source: *The Miami Herad, www. alexiscalatayud.com)*

I had the opportunity to speak with her and share some funny moments and war stories. I have no doubt that she will be around for a long time and achieve great things for South Florida!

NEW KIDS ON THE BLOCK

In January of 2000, I was relocated from Atlanta, Georgia, to Detroit, Michigan. It was a promotion, and I had a new role at Ford Motor Company which focused on philanthropy and not government affairs, therefore I was no longer responsible for political activities or lobbying. As a result, over the next few years, I sort of lost touch with Florida politics and the new crop of Cuban Americans who were being elected to the Florida Legislature and to local municipal offices.

Of course, I kept in touch with those who I had "grown up" in the process, and still do to this day. It's a bond that has lasted for over 30 years, and one that I am proud of and extremely grateful for.

With that said, I am so proud of the new wave of Cuban Americans elected (between 2000-2022) that followed the trailblazers. A few were legislative aides that I worked with, and it is awesome to see your friends achieve their dreams of being elected to public service.

Take my friend Esteban "Stevie" Bovo. He and I were legislative aides for many years. In 1998, he was elected to the Hialeah City Council, serving two terms. In 2008 he was elected to the Florida House of Representatives, where he served until March of 2011. From May of 2011 until November of 2020, he served as a member of the Miami-Dade County Commission. He served as Chair for the 2017/2018 term.

In November of 2021, Bovo was elected Mayor of the City of Hialeah, to serve a four-year term. He is the consummate public servant, putting people first.

Although I never had the opportunity to work with the majority of the second (or third) wave of Cuban Americans who went to Tallahassee, these leaders have really raised the bar, and that is certainly the case with Marco Antonio Rubio, who in November of 2006, made history as the 94th Speaker of the Florida House of Representatives and the first Cuban American to hold that office. Today, in his early fifties, Rubio represents Florida in the United States Senate as the Senior Senator since 2011.

A little more than a decade after Rubio, Jose Olivas (R-Hialeah) was elected Speaker of the Florida House, serving from November 20, 2018, to November 17, 2020. And, if all goes as planned, in November of 2024, Cuban American and Miami Republican Daniel Perez will become the third Cuban American to serve as Speaker of the Florida House, serving from 2024 to 2026. Perez currently represents Florida House District 116. Three Speakers of the Florida House in less than 20 years. Incredible!

FLORIDA'S SHIFTING HISPANIC DEMOGRAPHICS

Since January 1982, when Roberto Casas went to the Florida Legislature, a lot has changed. And a lot has not.

Cuba is still a communist country. The embargo is still law. Russia and

China, one could argue, are more powerful today than ever before because of their economic investments in Central and South America—not to mention in the U.S.

South Florida's Hispanic/Latino population constantly shifts a little less Cuban and more Central and South American. The next U.S. Census in 2030 will confirm this and, as a result, new political districts will be drawn. With that said, my guess is that Republican Cuban American legislators will be okay given it's the Florida Legislature that redraws their district lines. Central Florida is a different story.

As more and more Central and South Americans join Puerto Ricans in making Florida their home, and Central Florida at that, a shift will definitely occur. It is just a matter of time. According to a University of Central Florida thesis authored by Cynthia Melendez, *"Central Florida has seen the biggest jump in these numbers and now has more than 250,000 Hispanics of Puerto Rican origin making them the largest single group of Hispanics in the region. They now represent 49 percent of all Hispanics living in Central Florida."*

According to a 2017 *Florida Trend* article, *"Today, there are nearly 1.1 million Puerto Ricans living in Florida—roughly the same as in New York and more than twice as many as in any other U.S. state."* These 1.1 million Puerto Ricans have exerted their political muscle and, as a result, several Puerto Ricans have served in the Florida legislature and the U.S. Congress. They are also influential in state-wide races, such as governor. The majority of Puerto Ricans register Democrat, counter-balancing the Republican Cuban Americans in Miami.

Not every Hispanic elected official in Miami is Cuban. Although it may feel like that when reading this book, that is not the case. There have been other Hispanics elected to Congress, the state legislature, and local, municipal offices, such as Debbie Mucarsel-Powell (Ecuador), Annette Taddeo, and my friend Juan Carlos Zapata (both Colombian) to name a few.

Here's a perfect example of the shift. Maxwell Alejandro Frost is not your typical Cuban American. Elected to Congress in November 2022, Congressman Frost (D-Florida) is:

- The first member of Generation Z to serve in Congress.
- The first Afro-Cuban American to serve in Congress.
- The youngest member of Congress elected at the time, at age 25.

When Frost was 15, the Sandy Hook School shooting happened. That impacted his life in a meaningful way, so it is no surprise that the first piece of legislation he filed as a Member of Congress deals with gun violence. According to the proposed legislation, it would establish an Office of Gun Violence Prevention in the U.S. Department of Justice. "The Office of Gun Violence Prevention Act would bring together those most impacted by gun violence with leaders across federal agencies to advance policy, collect and report data, expand state and local outreach, and maximize existing programs and services related to preventing gun violence."

On March 22, 2023, this is what Frost said at the press conference introducing the proposed legislation, "As someone who grew up in a generation defined by mass shootings, an organizer to end this violent cycle since I was 15, and a survivor of gun violence myself, I came to Congress to continue the fight for a nation without fear, that's why I ensured this was the first legislation I introduced."

As Miami becomes more and more diverse with Colombians, Nicaraguans, and Venezuelans, along with others from Central and South America, these populations will aspire to and be elected to political and appointed offices. It is exactly what happened with the Haitian population in N.E. Miami-Dade.

Has the shift started? Change is happening every day. More and more South and Central Americans are coming to Miami-Dade County every day. We will need to wait until the 2030 Census and the 2032 reapportionment, when new districts will be re-drawn, to see the impact.

Certainly, in Doral (Miami-Dade County) and Weston (Broward County), Venezuelans dominate in population. Miami has a sizeable Nicaraguan population. According to a 2020 report by the Migration Policy Institute, more than 100,000 Venezuelans live in Miami-Dade County. It is the highest Venezuelan population of any metropolitan area in the United States. In 2022, Carolina Amesty, an American with

Venezuelan heritage, was elected State Representative, representing Florida's 45th district (Orlando area).

An August 2023 Pew Research study reported that between 2010 and 2021, the Venezuelan population in the U.S. increased by 169%, from roughly 240,000 to 640,000, researchers found. Dominicans and Guatemalans followed with growth rates of 60% each. While Mexicans remain the largest Latino origin group, they had the slowest growth rate at 13%.

According to Pew, the five largest Latino populations in the U.S. by origin group are: Mexicans (37.2 million), Puerto Ricans (5.8 million), Salvadorans (2.5 million), Dominicans (2.4 million) and Cubans (2.4 million).

This growth within the U.S. Latino population is not just a "Miami" factor. Take Los Angeles county as an example, as of 2021 there were 9.8 Million people. Of that total, 4.8 Million are Latino, with Mexican Americans comprising 74% of the Latino population. The remaining 26% are mostly from Central America, which is a trend that will continue to grow. My point here is that this change is happening, and it will continue to.

Back to Florida. According to Statista, as of 2020, close to 200,00 Columbians live in South Florida (Dade, Broward, and Palm Beach counties), with 115,000 calling Miami home. Miami-Dade County is home to 30% of Nicaraguans residing in the United States, which equates to over 120,000.

Little by little, Miami and Florida's political landscape when it comes to Hispanics is changing. With that said, Cuban American Republicans still have a stronghold when it comes to Florida politics and the reapportionment process, and probably will for the next two United States Census counts: 2030 and 2040. Please see Appendix C for a list of Cuban and Cuban Americans who followed the "firsts" to Tallahassee and Congress, the majority are registered Republicans.

THE IMPORTANCE OF BIPARTISANSHIP

Something that I have always been intentional about throughout my entire career is getting to know and working with individuals from "across the political' aisle. Regardless of my role as a public servant, political aide, corporate executive, nonprofit CEO, Chief Diversity Officer, and now as a consultant, I have always prided myself in being Bipartisan. It is so important to me. I see so much value in understanding how the other side thinks and why they think that way, and, more importantly, how we can work together.

As a Lobbyist at three Fortune 500 companies, it was very important to be bipartisan. Given all the complex issues that you deal with representing a large corporation, sometimes Republicans were on your side 100%, and sometimes it was the Democrats who got you over the finish line. In some states, maybe the legislature was from one party, yet the governor was from the opposite party.

During my first legislative session in Tallahassee, both houses of the Florida Legislature were run by Democrats: Bob Crawford served as Senate President and Tom Gustafson as Speaker of the Florida House. The Governor's office was held by Republican Bob Martinez.

In order to be effective as a lawmaker or staffer, I quickly realized that you had to be liked and respected by both sides. It was Democratic staffers who taught me how the Florida house worked. Why it was important to know and understand the rules, and most importantly, how the appropriations process worked in both the House and the Florida Senate.

It was not until 1998 that Florida's executive and legislative branches were governed by Republicans: Jeb Bush, Governor, Toni Jennings, Florida Senate President, and John Thrasher, Speaker of the Florida House. Cuban Americans from Miami and Florida have a reputation of being Republicans, and while that is certainly the case today and has been for a while, in the early years—late 1970s and early 1980s—many of the first Cuban Americans elected and appointed to office were Democrats. Republicans were struggling during that time period (think President Nixon, President Gerald Ford). These were the Jimmy Carter years, and Florida was governed by Democrats.

When former California Governor Ronald Reagan was elected President of the United States in 1980, many Cuban Americans started to switch their partly affiliation to Republican, given his strong opposition to Fidel Castro and Communism.

Some of you may be asking yourselves, why would Cuban Republicans want to work with Democrats? Because, when I worked in politics, bipartisanship existed. It was a good thing. One of my favorite sayings is: "Politics is the art of compromise." As such, Cuban Republicans from South Florida worked with Democrats. We worked together for the betterment of Miami-Dade County. If we did not, we would lose millions of state dollars to other counties. We worked together because we have things in common. Because it is good to have friends that may think and feel different than you, that have different experiences than you. I wish we could go back to those days of bipartisanship.

FRIENDSHIPS FROM ACROSS THE AISLE

Let me share a wonderful example of what I mean when I say, "working across the aisle."

Carrie Meek, the daughter of enslaved African Americans and sharecroppers, was the second African American women elected to the Florida House, the first African American woman elected to the Florida Senate (which is when I got to know her and her legislative aide, Opal Jones), and the first African American women elected to the United States House of Representatives since Reconstruction.

When Cuban Americans first arrived in Miami, Carrie is credited with helping hundreds of them, while she worked at Miami Dade Community College (now called Miami Dade College). Years later, when serving in the Florida Legislature, she had a wonderful friendship with Lincoln and Mario Díaz-Balart and Ileana Ros-Lehtinen which carried onto their service in Congress. In a Politico "postscript" piece, Ileana wrote this about Carrie Meek: "Carrie and I worked together on so many issues. She supported me on bills to help the Cuban people be free. I helped her on issues dealing with poverty and desperation in Haiti. For her — and for me — it was an American cause. And on bills helping to bring jobs and better education to Miami, there was no daylight between us."

One of the best people I've met, in and out of politics, is former Congressman Kendrick Brett Meek, Carrie Meek's baby boy. He and I have been friends since 1994, when my best friend in politics at the time, Alex Fernandez, introduced the two of us. Alex is the godfather of

Kendrick's son, KB, who today is in his mid-twenties. I volunteered for Kendrick's first campaign when he ran for state representative.

Prior to being elected to the Florida Legislature in 1994, Kendrick earned the rank of Captain in the Florida Highway Patrol and served as Florida Lieutenant Governor Buddy McKay's security detail. In 1998, Kendrick was elected to the Florida Senate, in the same district his mother, Carrie P. Meek, represented. In 2002, Kendrick once again succeeds his mother, this time in Congress, where he served four terms. In January 2009, Kendrick announced he would run for the United States Senate.

He made history by qualifying for the statewide ballot by petition, collecting over 112,000 signatures. Unfortunately, on November 2, 2010, Meek lost in a three-way-race against Governor Charlie Crist, and former Florida House Speaker Marco Rubio, who would go on to win the seat.

I think the world of Kendrick. It's been a friendship that has lasted almost 30 years, and one I hope to have until the good Lord calls me. I am hoping that Kendrick decides to either seek public office, or is appointed to a political office once again. We need leaders like Kendrick in public service. Bipartisanship is good for individuals, good for the soul, and good for this country.

Kendrick Meek, Rocky Egusquiza and me, circa 1996, taken in Tallahassee at an event celebrating his re-election. (Photo courtesy of Kendrick Meek)

IN CLOSING...

I hope you have enjoyed reading this book as much as I have enjoyed writing it. I am proud of it. I am fortunate to have been able to meet and work with most of the elected and appointed officials included in the book—Republicans, Democrats, Independents. It really is my "love letter" to them. All of them, and so many others that have added tremendous value, purpose, and meaning to my life. Whether I agreed with them or not, they have made me think differently. Asked me to see "the other side" of an issue, which has made me a better lobbyist, corporate executive, and nonprofit leader: the three hats I've proudly worn professionally for the last 30+ years. Ultimately, they have made me a better leader and human being.

(Photo Credit: iStock/azatvaleev)

CARLOS F. ORTA
Condensed Biography

Carlos, the only child of Carlos and Maria L. Orta, was born in June 1966, in Havana, Cuba. He and his family emigrated from Cuba to Spain, where they sought political asylum. In August of 1971, they made it to America and settled in Miami, Florida, where Carlos grew up. Not speaking a word of English and his parents working 3-4 jobs, the first few years were a struggle.

His foray into politics at the age of 21 began unexpectedly with an internship offer from a high school friend, leading to an impactful career. Carlos quickly rose through the ranks, excelling in political campaigns and serving as a legislative aide before transitioning to the corporate world as a lobbyist for several Fortune 500 companies. Transitioning to the nonprofit world, Orta's leadership continued as he led the Hispanic Association on Corporate Responsibility in Washington, D.C., for eight years, advocating for Latino representation in corporate America.

All these diverse experiences fueled his passion for writing and led to the publication of his book—a reflection of his time working alongside trailblazers and history makers. Carlos is now based in Washington, D.C., with his wife, Mary Ann Gomez. He cherishes the opportunity to connect with readers and peers, anticipating new learnings, friends, and experiences, just as he did when he first came to America.

WORKS CITED

- "1980." Bill Clinton Museum. 2024. https://clintonhousemuseum. org/announcement/bc-1980/
- Benesch, Susan and Rick Bragg. "Not Just a War of Words." *Tampa Bay Times.* March 29, 1992. https://www.tampabay.com/ archive/1992/03/29/not-just-a-war-of-words/
- Cohen, Howard. "Jorge Valdes, first Hispanic on Miami-Dade Commission, dies at 74." Local Obituaries, Miami Herald. October 21, 2014. https://www.miamiherald.com/news/local/obituaries/ article3213701.html
- "Cuban-Born Commissioner Is Elected Mayor of Miami." *The New York Times.* July 25, 1996. https://www.nytimes.com/1996/07/25/us/ cuban-born-commissioner-is-elected-mayor-of-miami.html
- "Cuban Independence." Cubans in America. Accessed March 22, 2024. https://cubansinamerica.us/web/history-of-cuba/cuban- independence/.
- "Cubans Vote Felt in Miami Election." *The New York Times.* November 18, 1973. https://www.nytimes.com/1973/11/18/archives/ cubans-vote-felt-in-miami-election-winners-are-democrats-termed. html
- "Former Hialeah Candidate Charged with Viter Fraud." *Sun Sentinel.* September 18, 2004. https://www.sun-sentinel.com/2004/09/18/ former-hialeah-candidate-charged-with-voter-fraud/
- Frost, Maxwell Alejandro and Chris Murphy. "Office of Gun Violence Prevention Act." 2023. https://www.murphy.senate.gov/ imo/media/doc/office_of_gvp_one_pager.pdf
- Geiling, Natasha. "Before the Revolution: Socialites and Celebrities Flocked to Cuba." *Smithsonian Magazine.* July 31, 2007. https://www.smithsonianmag.com/history/before-the- revolution159682020/#:~:text=In%20Cuba%2C%20they%20 could%20continue,millions%20of%20dollars%20every%20month
- "Grau San Martin, Prio and Batista." Cubans in America. Accessed March 22, 2024. https://cubansinamerica.us/web/history-of-cuba/ grau-san-martin-prio-and-batista/.

- History.com Editors, "Cuban Missile Crisis." History Channel. https://www.history.com/topics/cold-war/cuban-missile-crisis
- Melendez, Cynthia. "The Emergence of Central Florida's Puerto Rican Community" (2007). *Electronic Theses and Dissertations*. 3263. https://stars.library.ucf.edu/etd/3263
- Olasov, Ian. "Offensive Political Dog Whistles: You know them When you Hear them. Or do you?" *Vox*. November 7, 2016. https://www.vox.com/the-big-idea/2016/11/7/13549154/dog-whistles-campaign-racism
- PBS Staff. "Cuban Exiles in America." *American Experience*. 2005. https://www.pbs.org/wgbh/americanexperience/features/castro-cuban-exiles-america/
- Ros-Lehtinen, Ileana. "Carrie Meek: A Pioneering Congresswoman Who Befriended Political Foes." *Politico*. December 17, 2021. https://www.politico.com/news/magazine/2021/12/27/2021-obituary-carrie-meek-520597
- "The Bay of Pigs and the Cuban Missile Crisis, 1961-1962." U.S. Department of State. https://20012009.state.gov/r/pa/ho/time/ea/17739.htm#:~:text=After%20much%20debate%20in%20his,spectacular%20failure%20within%202%20days.
- "Title XVII -- Cuban Democracy Act of 1992." U.S. Department of State. https://1997-2001.state.gov/www/regions/wha/cuba/democ_act_1992.html
- "Tuesday's Afternoon Update." *Florida Trend*. December 12, 2017. https://www.floridatrend.com/article/23564/tuesdays-afternoon-update
- "UF Celebrates Program Aimed at Educating Exiled Cuban Lawyers." Florida Bar News. October 1, 2015. https://www.floridabar.org/the-florida-bar-news/uf-celebrates-program-aimed-at-educating-exiled-cuban-lawyers/
- Yanez, Luisa, Carol Rosenberg, Matthew I. Pinzur and Scott Hiassen. "Ex-commissioner Kills Himself in Lobby." Miami Herald. July 28, 2005. https://miamiarchives.blogspot.com/2012/07/july-27-2005-arthur-teele-kills-himself.html

APPENDIX A

Cuban Americans elected to the Florida Legislature from 1982-1990.

1982 Florida House:
1. Roberto Casas (R-Hialeah)
2. Ileana Ros Lehtinen (R-Miami)
3. Humberto Cortina (R-Little Havana)

1984 Florida House:
1. Roberto Casas (R-Hialeah)
2. Ileana Ros Lehtinen (R-Miami)
3. Luis C. Morse (R-Little Havana)
4. Arnhilda Badia (R-Miami)
5. Alberto "Al" Gutman (R-Miami
6. Javier Souto (R-Miami)

1985 Florida House:
1. Rudy Garcia (R-Hialeah)

1986 Florida House:
1. Roberto Casas (R-Hialeah)
2. Arnhilda Badia (R-Miami)
3. Alberto "Al" Gutman (R-Miami)
4. Javier Souto (R-Miami)
5. Luis C. Morse (R- Little Havana)
6. Rudy Garcia (R-Hialeah)
7. Lincoln Díaz-Balart (R-Miami)

1986 Florida Senate:
1. Ileana Ros Lehtinen (R-Miami)

1988 Florida Senate:
1. Roberto Casas (R-Hialeah)
2. Ileana Ros Lehtinen (R-Miami)
3. Javier Souto (R-Miami)

1988 Florida House:
1. Alberto "Al" Gutman (R-Miami)

2. Luis C. Morse (R-Little Havana)
3. Lincoln Díaz-Balart (R-Miami)
4. Mario Díaz-Balart (R-Miami)
5. Nilo Juri (R-Hialeah)
6. Luis Rojas (R-Hialeah)
7. Carlos Valdez (R-West Miami)

1989 Florida Senate:
1. Roberto Casas (R-Hialeah)
2. Ileana Ros Lehtinen (R-Miami) (Resigned August 1989)
3. Lincoln Díaz-Balart (R-Miami) (Elected August 1989)
4. Javier Souto (R-West Dade)

1989 Florida House:
1. Alberto "Al" Gutman (R-Miami)
2. Luis C. Morse (R-Little Havana)
3. Rudy Garcia (R-Hialeah) (Elected November 7, 1989)
4. Miguel De Grandy, (R-Miami)
5. Mario Díaz-Balart, (R-Miami)
6. Nilo Juri (R-Hialeah) (Resigned Summer 1989)
7. Luis Rojas (R-Hialeah)
8. Carlos Valdez (R-West Miami)

1990 Florida House:
1. Alberto "Al" Gutman (R-Miami)
2. Luis C. Morse (R-Little Havana)
3. Rudy Garcia (R-Hialeah)
4. Miguel De Grandy, (R-Miami)
5. Mario Díaz-Balart, (R-Miami)
6. Luis Rojas (R-Hialeah)
7. Carlos Valdez (R-West Miami)

1990 Florida Senate:
1. Roberto Casas (R-Hialeah)
2. Lincoln Díaz-Balart (R-Miami)
3. Javier Souto (R-West Dade)

APPENDIX B

Cuban Americans elected (and re-elected) to the Florida Legislature from 1992-2000:

1992 Florida House:
1. Bruno Barreiro (R-Miami Beach)
2. Alex Villalobos (R-West Dade)
3. Eladio Armesto Garcia (R-Little Havana)
4. Carlos Manrique (R-West Dade)
5. Luis C. Morse (R-Little Havana)
6. Rudy Garcia (R-Hialeah)
7. Miguel De Grandy, (R-Miami)
8. Luis Rojas (R-Hialeah)
9. Carlos Valdez (R-West Miami)

1992 Florida Senate:
1. Roberto Casas (R-Hialeah)
2. Alberto Gutman (R-Miami Beach)
3. Mario Díaz-Balart (R-West Dade)

1994 Florida House:
1. Alex Díaz de la Portilla (R-West Dade)
2. Annie Betancourt (D- West Dade)
3. Jorge Rodriguez-Chomat (R-Miami)
4. Carlos Lacasa (R-Coral Gables)
5. Bruno Barreiro (R-Miami Beach)
6. Alex Villalobos (R-West Dade)
7. Luis C. Morse (R-Little Havana)
8. Rudy Garcia (R-Hialeah)
9. Luis Rojas (R-Hialeah)
10. Carlos Valdez (R-West Miami)

1994 Florida Senate:
10. Roberto Casas (R-Hialeah)
11. Alberto Gutman (R-Miami Beach)
12. Mario Díaz-Balart (R-West Dade)
7. Lincoln Díaz-Balart (R-Miami)

1996 Florida House:
1. Alex Díaz de la Portilla (R-West Dade)
2. Annie Betancourt (D-West Dade)
3. Jorge Rodriguez-Chomat (R-Miami)
4. Carlos Lacasa (R-Coral Gables)
5. Bruno Barreiro (R-Miami Beach)
6. Alex Villalobos (R-West Dade)
7. Luis C. Morse (R-Little Havana)
8. Rudy Garcia (R-Hialeah)
9. Luis Rojas (R-Hialeah)
10. Carlos Valdez (R-West Miami)

1996 Florida Senate:
1. Roberto Casas (R-Hialeah)
2. Alberto Gutman (R-Miami Beach)
3. Mario Díaz-Balart (R-West Dade)

1998 Florida House:
1. Manuel Prieguez (R-Little Havana)
2. Gaston Cantens (R-West Dade)
3. Gustavo Barreiro (R-Miami)
4. Alex Diaz de la Portilla (R-Miami)
5. Annie Betancourt (D-West Dade)
6. Carlos Lacasa (R-Coral Gables)
7. Alex Villalobos (R-West Dade)
8. Rudy Garcia (R-Hialeah)
9. Luis Rojas (R-Hialeah)
10. Carlos Valdez (R-West Miami)

1998 Florida Senate:
1. Roberto Casas (R-Hialeah)
2. Alberto Gutman (R-Miami Beach)
3. Mario Díaz-Balart (R-West Dade)

2000 Florida House:
1. Rafael Arza (R-Miami)
2. Renier Díaz de la Portilla (R-Miami)
3. Rene Garcia (R-Hialeah)
4. Marco Antonio Rubio (R-West Miami)

5. Mario Díaz-Balart (R-West Dade)
6. Manuel Prieguez (R-Little Havana)
7. Gaston Cantens (R-West Miami)
8. Gustavo Barreiro (R-Miami)
9. Annie Betancourt (D-West Dade)
10. Carlos Lacasa (R-Coral Gables)

2000 Florida Senate:
1. Rudy Garcia (R-Hialeah)
2. Alex Villalobos (R-West Dade)
3. Alex Díaz de la Portilla (R-West Dade)

APPENDIX C

Cuban and Cuban Americans who followed the "firsts" to Tallahassee and Congress. As you will see, the majority are registered Republicans with some exception, (D).

Florida Senate: 2000 – 2022
1. Alex Díaz de le Portilla
2. Rene Garcia
3. Anitere Flores
4. Miguel Díaz de la Portilla
5. Frank Artiles
6. Jose Javier Rodriguez (D)
7. Manny Díaz
8. Ana Maria Rodriguez
9. Ileana Garcia
10. Alexis Calatayud
11. Bryan Avila

Florida House of Representatives: 2000 – 2022
1. Frank Artiles
2. Rafael Arza
3. Gustavo Barreiro
4. Annie Betancourt (D)
5. Michael Bileca
6. Esteban Bovo
7. Gaston Cantens
8. Jose Felix Díaz
9. Renier Díaz de la Portilla
10. Nicolas Duran (D)
11. Anitere Flores
12. Erik Fresen
13. Luis Garcia, Jr. (D)
14. Rene Garcia
15. Eduardo Gonzalez
16. Vicky Lopez
17. Carlos Lopez-Cantera
18. Marcelo Llorente
19. Jeanette Nuñez

20. Jose Olivas
21. Daniel Perez, Speaker Designate (2024-2026)
22. Juan Carlos Planas
23. Manuel Prieguez
24. Ana Rivas Logan
25. David Rivera
26. Julio Robaina
27. Marco Rubio
28. Carlos Trujillo

United States Congress: 2000 – 2022
1. David Rivera (R-Miami, 2011-2013)
2. Joe Garcia (D-Miami, 2013-2015)
3. Carlos Curbelo (R-Miami, 2015-2019)
4. Carlos Giménez (R-Miami, 2021-present)
5. Debbie Mucarsel-Powell (D-Miami, 2019-2021)
6. Maria Elvira Salazar (R-Miami, 2021-present)

United States Senate: (2000 – 2022)
1. Mel Martinez (R-Orlando, 2005-2009)
2. Marco Rubio (R-Miami, 2011-present)

www.ingramcontent.com/pod-product-compliance
Lightning Source LLC
Chambersburg PA
CBHW051311120626
46547CB00015B/2191